CYBERSECURITY
MASTERCLASS

The Ultimate 15-Step Blueprint
for Aspiring Professionals

TONY EVANS

ISBN: 979-8-218-50571-4
First Edition, 2024

Published by PROFYLE PUBLISHING LLC
Atlanta, GA

Printed in the United States

Disclaimer
This book is for educational purposes, based on personal experiences and research conducted during the teaching of cybersecurity. The author and publisher have made every effort to ensure the accuracy of the information presented, but no legal responsibility is assumed for errors, omissions, or discrepancies.

Table of Contents

Table of Contents

INTRODUCTION

The purpose of this book is to simplify the complexities of cybersecurity into clear, digestible concepts. My goal is to provide a structured, step-by-step approach to understanding the key domains, technologies, and best practices in cybersecurity. This book will not only explain what cybersecurity entails but also why it matters, using real-world examples and case studies to highlight its significance. You don't need a deep technical background to grasp the concepts presented, as we will start from the fundamentals and gradually build your knowledge. I will also break down common cybersecurity terms and technologies, providing clear definitions and explanations throughout the book. Beyond that, this book offers practical guidance on developing essential cybersecurity skills and gaining hands-on experience—the kind of guidance I wish I had when I graduated from Kennesaw State with my Master's Degree.

As I reflect on my journey, it's been an incredible story. I was working at Amazon delivering packages when my Dad mentioned he had a G.I. Bill available for his kids to go back to school. At the time, I already had a Bachelor's Degree in Marketing, but the pandemic made it difficult to navigate my way into a career. After doing some research, I told my dad I wanted to use the G.I. Bill to pursue a Master's Degree in cybersecurity. The term "cybersecurity" had been floating around, and it aligned with my interests. Growing up, I was always the one fixing technology, helping people with their networks, securing their internet, hacking into applications, and downloading illegal software. The field intrigued me, and it seemed like a career with a promising future, so I decided to give it a try.

INTRODUCTION

I considered enrolling at Western Governors University, but I found the cost to be higher than Kennesaw State, and I also needed to obtain the CompTIA Security+ certification before starting classes. At the time, I was new to the field and didn't have the confidence to secure the certification within the two-month timeframe before classes began, so I decided to start my journey at Kennesaw State instead. At Kennesaw State, I could use my G.I. Bill right away and begin the foundational courses, which is when I realized that I was going to excel in cybersecurity.

After completing the foundational courses, I spent a full year in the Master's program at Kennesaw State, which I found to be both unique and enjoyable. One of the assignments I particularly enjoyed was leading all aspects of our Capstone project, where I demonstrated my leadership skills. I coordinated with team members, scheduled meetings, and provided regular updates. Together, we developed several deliverables, including a Security Services Plan, Policy Program Design, Information Security Policy, Governance Staffing Plan, and a practical, cloud-based threat intelligence and analytics system on Amazon Web Services. This project emphasized identifying and patching cloud security vulnerabilities through comprehensive analysis of cloud-specific data and adversarial tactics.

In addition, I implemented a Caesar Cipher in Python, conducted a digital forensics investigation, and created a risk management table where I ranked assets for a company. These experiences solidified my passion for cybersecurity and deepened my understanding of the field.

INTRODUCTION

Due to the hype surrounding cybersecurity, I assumed that simply having a Master's Degree would guarantee me a job in the field after graduation. I quickly learned that I was competing against literally millions of applicants with more expertise than I had. While in school, I didn't complete any internships or earn certifications, which I hadn't realized were essential at the time. Now, as an instructor, I stress the importance of gaining experience while still in school. I wish I had someone like myself to guide me back then.

At the time of my graduation, I was still working at Square as a Customer Service Representative, and I struggled to navigate the cybersecurity job market. My resume mainly highlighted my Master's Degree from Kennesaw State but lacked the additional expertise needed to stand out. I turned to networking within my company, using Slack channels to connect with colleagues. I posted in all the information security and cybersecurity channels, mentioning that I had just graduated with a Master's Degree and was seeking any available roles or shadowing opportunities.

My first break came when I received responses to my message, allowing me to start shadowing in the Information Security department and on the Detection, Alert, and Response team. At that point, I still didn't have any certifications and was focused on gaining hands-on experience to see if I could advance within the company. Feeling a bit impatient, I continued applying for other jobs to improve my career and financial situation.

INTRODUCTION

During my job search, I came across a Cybersecurity Instructor position at Chattahoochee Tech. To be completely honest, I never imagined I would become a teacher. While I was always intelligent and good at presenting and breaking down information for others, teaching was never something I had considered, given how I was in school. However, I excelled in the interview, confidently expressing my passion for cybersecurity and my ability to mentor students and design educational materials. Within 24 hours, I received an offer from Chattahoochee Tech, and the rest is history.

What truly motivated me to write this book was seeing things from the students' perspective. Many of them, being around my age, approach me with questions about how to get jobs, structure their resumes, what opportunities are out there, and how the material we learn in class applies to the real world. I realized that I needed to provide this information not only to my students but also to self-taught individuals and non-traditional learners looking to make a career change, just like I did.

When I started my journey in cybersecurity, I didn't have anyone to guide me or tell me what steps to take. Now, I feel a sense of responsibility to help the next generation of security leaders by providing the information they need. My hope is that readers will use this book as a valuable resource to guide their own cybersecurity journeys. It's packed with game and advice, so I'm sure you'll find it helpful. Feel free to thank me later!

CHAPTER ONE

Cybersecurity Landscape

CHAPTER ONE OBJECTIVES

After reading this chapter, the reader will be able to:

- Comprehend the fundamental concepts and terminology related to cybersecurity.
- Appreciate the importance of cybersecurity in today's digital landscape.
- Identify the various types of cyber threats and their potential impact.
- Understand the key principles and best practices for mitigating cyber risks.
- Recognize the role of cybersecurity professionals and the diverse career opportunities available.
- Develop a solid foundation for further exploration and mastery of cybersecurity principles.

CYBERSECURITY LANDSCAPE

A. Definition of Cybersecurity

Cybersecurity refers to the practice of protecting computer systems, networks, programs, and data from digital attacks, unauthorized access, theft, damage, disruption, or misdirection. It involves implementing various security measures to ensure the confidentiality, integrity, and availability of information assets.

B. The Evolution of Cybersecurity Threats and Challenges

The cybersecurity landscape has undergone significant changes over the years, with threats becoming more sophisticated and diverse. In the early days of computing, threats were primarily limited to computer viruses and worms. However, as technology advanced and the internet became more widespread, the nature of cyber threats evolved. Today, organizations face a wide range of threats, including targeted attacks, advanced persistent threats, ransomware, and social engineering techniques like phishing. The increasing complexity of IT infrastructures, the increase of connected devices, and the growing reliance on cloud services have further expanded the attack surface, making it more challenging to secure.

CYBERSECURITY DOMAINS AND CAREER PATH

Cybersecurity is a broad field that encompasses various domains, each with its own set of skills, tools, and methodologies. This section will explore some of the key domains and the associated career paths.

 A. Information Security

Information security focuses on protecting the confidentiality, integrity, and availability of data. Professionals in this domain are responsible for designing and implementing security policies, procedures, and controls to safeguard sensitive information from unauthorized access or modification. They assess risks, develop security architectures, and ensure compliance with industry standards and regulations.

Career paths in information security include:

- Information Security Analyst: Responsible for identifying and mitigating security risks, conducting vulnerability assessments, and monitoring security events.
- Security Architect: Designs and oversees the implementation of an organization's security infrastructure, ensuring that it aligns with business objectives and regulatory requirements.
- Security Engineer: Develops and implements security solutions, such as firewalls, intrusion detection systems, and access control mechanisms.

CYBERSECURITY DOMAINS AND CAREER PATH

B. Network Security

Network security involves protecting an organization's computer networks and infrastructure from cyber threats. Network security professionals are responsible for designing, implementing, and maintaining secure network architectures, as well as monitoring and responding to security incidents. They configure and manage network security devices, such as firewalls and intrusion prevention systems, and ensure that network traffic is properly segmented and controlled.

Career paths in network security include:

- Network Security Engineer: Designs and implements secure network architectures, configures security devices, and troubleshoots network security issues.
- Network Security Administrator: Responsible for the day-to-day management and monitoring of an organization's network security infrastructure.
- Firewall Administrator: Configures and manages firewall systems to control network traffic and prevent unauthorized access.

CYBERSECURITY DOMAINS AND CAREER PATH

C. Cloud Security

As organizations increasingly adopt cloud computing, ensuring the security of cloud-based assets has become a critical concern. Cloud security professionals are responsible for securing cloud infrastructures, platforms, and applications, as well as ensuring compliance with relevant security standards and regulations. They work closely with cloud service providers to implement security controls, monitor for threats, and respond to incidents.

Career paths in cloud security include:

- Cloud Security Architect: Designs and implements secure cloud architectures, ensuring that they meet security and compliance requirements.
- Cloud Security Engineer: Configures and manages security controls for cloud environments, monitors for security events, and responds to incidents.
- Cloud Security Consultant: Provides expert advice and guidance to organizations on securing their cloud deployments and ensuring compliance with industry standards.

CYBERSECURITY DOMAINS AND CAREER PATH

D. Application Security

Application security focuses on identifying, preventing, and mitigating security vulnerabilities in software applications. Professionals in this domain are responsible for secure coding practices, vulnerability assessments, and penetration testing to ensure the security of applications throughout their lifecycle. They work closely with development teams to integrate security into the software development process and provide guidance on secure coding practices.

Career paths in application security include:

- Application Security Engineer: Conducts security assessments and penetration testing of applications, identifies vulnerabilities, and provides recommendations for remediation.
- Secure Software Developer: Develops software applications using secure coding practices and ensures that security is integrated throughout the development lifecycle.
- Application Security Analyst: Analyzes application security risks, conducts code reviews, and provides guidance on secure coding practices.

CYBERSECURITY DOMAINS AND CAREER PATH

E. Incident Response and Forensics

Incident response and forensics professionals are responsible for detecting, investigating, and responding to security incidents and breaches. They use various tools and techniques to identify the root cause of incidents, contain the damage, and recover systems and data. They also collect and analyze evidence to support legal proceedings and improve an organization's security posture.

Career paths in incident response and forensics include:

- Incident Response Analyst: Triages and investigates security incidents, coordinates response efforts, and communicates with stakeholders.
- Digital Forensics Investigator: Collects and analyzes digital evidence to support investigations and legal proceedings.
- Security Operations Center (SOC) Analyst: Monitors security events, detects and responds to threats, and provides real-time analysis and incident coordination.

CYBERSECURITY DOMAINS AND CAREER PATH

F. Penetration Testing and Ethical Hacking

Penetration testers, also known as ethical hackers, simulate real-world cyberattacks to identify vulnerabilities in an organization's networks, systems, and applications. They use the same tools and techniques as malicious hackers but with permission and for the purpose of improving security. They provide organizations with valuable insights into their security posture and help prioritize remediation efforts.

Career paths in penetration testing and ethical hacking include:

- Penetration Tester: Conducts authorized simulated attacks on an organization's systems and networks to identify vulnerabilities and provide recommendations for remediation.
- Ethical Hacker: Uses hacking techniques and tools to assess the security of an organization's systems and applications, providing insights into potential weaknesses.
- Red Team: Works as part of a team to simulate advanced, persistent threats and test an organization's detection and response capabilities.

CYBERSECURITY DOMAINS AND CAREER PATH

G. Cybersecurity Governance and Compliance

Cybersecurity governance and compliance professionals ensure that an organization's security practices align with relevant laws, regulations, and industry standards. They develop and implement security policies, conduct risk assessments, and oversee compliance audits. They work closely with senior management to ensure that security objectives are aligned with business goals and that the organization is meeting its legal and regulatory obligations.

Career paths in cybersecurity governance and compliance include:

- Information Security Manager: Develops and oversees the implementation of an organization's security policies and procedures, ensuring alignment with business objectives and regulatory requirements.
- Compliance Officer: Ensures that an organization's security practices comply with relevant laws, regulations, and industry standards, and manages compliance audits and assessments.
- Risk Manager: Identifies, assesses, and mitigates security risks to an organization's assets, operations, and reputation.

CYBERSECURITY DOMAINS AND CAREER PATH

H. Cybersecurity Management and Leadership

Cybersecurity management and leadership roles involve overseeing an organization's overall security strategy and operations. These professionals are responsible for managing security teams, budgets, and resources, as well as communicating with stakeholders and ensuring alignment with business objectives. They provide strategic direction, develop and implement security programs, and ensure that an organization's security posture is continuously improving.

Career paths in cybersecurity management and leadership include:

- Chief Information Security Officer (CISO): Leads an organization's overall security strategy, manages security teams and budgets, and communicates with senior management and the board of directors.
- Security Director: Oversees the development and implementation of an organization's security programs, manages security operations, and ensures alignment with business objectives.
- Cybersecurity Program Manager: Manages the planning, execution, and delivery of specific security projects and initiatives, ensuring that they are completed on time, within budget, and to the required quality standards.

CYBERSECURITY TRENDS AND EMERGING THREATS

As the cybersecurity landscape continues to evolve, it is essential for aspiring professionals to stay informed about the latest trends and emerging threats. This section will highlight some of the key trends and threats to watch out for in the coming years.

A. Evolving Ransomware Attacks

Ransomware attackers are increasingly targeting critical infrastructure, such as healthcare facilities, energy providers, and transportation systems, to maximize the impact of their attacks and increase the likelihood of ransom payments.

Attackers are using double extortion tactics, where they not only encrypt an organization's data but also threaten to release sensitive information if the ransom is not paid. The rise of ransomware-as-a-service models has also made it easier for less skilled attackers to launch ransomware campaigns.

B. Supply Chain and Third-Party Risk

Attackers are targeting software supply chains, compromising widely used libraries, frameworks, and dependencies to distribute malware and gain access to multiple organizations.

Organizations are increasingly relying on third-party vendors and managed service providers, which can introduce additional security risks if these parties do not have adequate security controls in place.

CYBERSECURITY TRENDS AND EMERGING THREATS

C. Cloud Security Challenges

Misconfigurations and insecure cloud deployments, such as exposed storage buckets and misconfigured access controls, can lead to data breaches and unauthorized access to sensitive information.

The increasing use of distributed cloud environments and multi-cloud strategies can introduce complexity and make it more challenging to maintain consistent security controls across different platforms and providers.

D. Artificial Intelligence and Machine Learning in Cybersecurity

Attackers are leveraging AI and ML techniques to automate and scale their attacks, evade detection, and adapt to defenses. Adversarial machine learning techniques are being used to manipulate and deceive AI-based security systems.

Organizations are increasingly using AI and ML to enhance their threat detection and response capabilities, automate security processes, and identify anomalies and potential threats in real-time.

CYBERSECURITY TRENDS AND EMERGING THREATS

E. Popular Sources for Staying Up-to-Date

Reports such as the Verizon Data Breach Investigations Report provide valuable insights into the latest trends, attack patterns, and best practices in cybersecurity.

Blogs and online communities, such as the SANS Internet Storm Center, offer timely analysis, news, and discussions on current cybersecurity topics and emerging threats.

Conferences and events, such as the RSA Conference and Black Hat, provide opportunities to learn from industry experts, network with peers, and stay up-to-date on the latest developments in the field.

CHAPTER TWO

Master Security Fundamentals

CHAPTER TWO OBJECTIVES

After reading this chapter, the reader will be able to:

- Understand the key components of computer hardware, operating systems, and networking
- Explain the core information security principles, including the CIA triad and the concepts of threats, vulnerabilities, and risks
- Develop a security mindset and adopt a proactive approach to security
- Identify and implement security policies, standards, and compliance frameworks
- Apply access controls and authentication models to secure systems and data
- Grasp the basic concepts of cryptography, including encryption, hashing, and digital signatures

KEY COMPUTING BASICS

A. Computer Hardware

Computer hardware consists of various components, each serving a specific function. The main components include the central processing unit (CPU) which executes instructions and performs calculations, random access memory (RAM) which temporarily stores data and instructions, and storage devices such as hard disk drives (HDDs) and solid-state drives (SSDs), which provide long-term storage for data and programs.

Interfaces, such as USB, HDMI, and Ethernet, allow computers to communicate with external devices and networks. Peripherals, such as keyboards, mice, and printers, enable users to interact with computers and perform input and output tasks.

B. Operating Systems

Operating systems (OS) are software that manage computer hardware, software, and provide a user interface. Common types of operating systems include Windows, macOS, Linux, iOS, and Android. Each OS has its own unique features, user interface, and security considerations.

Operating systems play a critical role in computing and security. They control access to system resources, manage user permissions, and provide a platform for running applications. Secure configuration and regular updates of operating systems are essential for maintaining the security of computing devices.

KEY COMPUTING BASICS

C. Networking Fundamentals

Networks can be classified into different types, such as local area networks (LANs), wide area networks (WANs), and wireless networks (WLANs). Network topologies, such as bus, star, and mesh, define the physical or logical layout of a network and how devices are connected.

Network protocols are sets of rules that govern communication between devices on a network. The Open Systems Interconnection (OSI) model is a conceptual framework that divides network communication into seven layers, each responsible for specific functions, such as data encoding, routing, and application-level services.

KEY COMPUTING BASICS

D. Virtualization

Virtualization is the process of creating virtual versions of computing resources, such as servers, storage, and networks. It allows multiple virtual machines (VMs) to run on a single physical host, improving resource utilization, flexibility, and scalability.

Hypervisors are software that manage and allocate resources to virtual machines. There are two main types of hypervisors: Type 1 (bare-metal) and Type 2 (hosted). Virtual machines are software-based emulations of physical computers, each with its own operating system, applications, and virtual hardware.

While virtualization offers many benefits, it also introduces new security challenges. These include securing the hypervisor, isolating virtual machines, and managing access to shared resources. Proper configuration, monitoring, and security controls are essential to maintain the security of virtualized environments.

CORE INFORMATION SECURITY POLICIES

A. The CIA Triad

Confidentiality ensures that information is accessible only to authorized individuals or systems. It involves protecting sensitive data from unauthorized disclosure through access controls, encryption, and secure communication channels.

Integrity refers to the accuracy, consistency, and trustworthiness of data throughout its lifecycle. It ensures that information is not altered, destroyed, or corrupted, either accidentally or maliciously. Integrity controls, such as hashing and digital signatures, help maintain the integrity of data.

Availability ensures that information and systems are accessible and operational when needed by authorized users. It involves protecting against disruptions, such as hardware failures, network outages, and denial-of-service attacks, and implementing measures like redundancy, backup, and disaster recovery.

CORE INFORMATION SECURITY POLICIES

B. Threats, Vulnerabilities, and Risks

A threat is a potential cause of harm to a system or organization, such as a malicious actor, natural disaster, or human error. A vulnerability is a weakness in a system or control that can be exploited by a threat. Risk is the potential impact of a threat exploiting a vulnerability, considering the likelihood and consequences of the event.

Common types of threats include malware (viruses, worms, trojans), phishing attacks, insider threats, and advanced persistent threats (APTs). Each type of threat has its own characteristics, attack vectors, and potential impacts on an organization.

Vulnerability and risk assessment are essential processes in cybersecurity. They involve identifying and evaluating the vulnerabilities in a system or organization, assessing the potential impact of threats exploiting those vulnerabilities, and prioritizing remediation efforts based on the level of risk.

CORE INFORMATION SECURITY POLICIES

C. The Security Mindset

Adopting a security mindset requires thinking like an attacker. This involves understanding the motivations, techniques, and tactics used by malicious actors to identify potential weaknesses and attack vectors in a system or organization.

A proactive approach to security focuses on preventing incidents before they occur, rather than simply reacting to them after the fact. This involves implementing security controls, monitoring for threats, and continuously improving security posture based on emerging risks and best practices.

The cybersecurity landscape is constantly evolving, with new threats, technologies, and best practices emerging regularly. Continuous learning and adaptation are essential for staying ahead of the curve and maintaining effective security. This involves staying informed about the latest trends, participating in training and certification programs, and collaborating with peers and experts in the field.

SECURITY POLICIES AND COMPLIANCE

A. Security Policies

Security policies are documents that define an organization's approach to information security. They establish the rules, responsibilities, and expectations for protecting sensitive data and systems. Types of security policies include acceptable use policies, access control policies, incident response policies, and data classification policies.

Developing effective security policies involves understanding an organization's business objectives, legal and regulatory requirements, and risk tolerance. Policies should be clear, concise, and enforceable, and should be regularly reviewed and updated to ensure their relevance. Implementing security policies requires communication, training, and monitoring to ensure compliance.

SECURITY POLICIES AND COMPLIANCE

B. Security Standards

Security standards provide best practices and guidelines for implementing security controls in specific industries or contexts. Examples include the ISO 27001 standard for information security management, the NIST Cybersecurity Framework for critical infrastructure, and the Payment Card Industry Data Security Standard (PCI-DSS) for organizations handling credit card data.

Best practices and guidelines provide recommendations for implementing security controls based on industry experience and consensus. They cover a wide range of topics, such as password policies, network segmentation, and incident response procedures. Following best practices and guidelines can help organizations align with industry standards and improve their overall security posture.

SECURITY POLICIES AND COMPLIANCE

C. Compliance Frameworks

Regulatory requirements are legal obligations that organizations must comply with to operate in specific industries or jurisdictions. Examples include the General Data Protection Regulation (GDPR) for organizations handling personal data of European Union citizens, and the Health Insurance Portability and Accountability Act (HIPAA) for organizations handling protected health information in the United States.

Compliance audits and assessments are processes that evaluate an organization's adherence to regulatory requirements and industry standards. They involve reviewing documentation, interviewing personnel, and testing controls to identify gaps and areas for improvement. Regular compliance audits and assessments help ensure that organizations maintain a strong security posture and avoid legal and financial penalties.

ACCESS CONTROLS AND AUTHENTICATION

A. Types of Access Controls

Physical access controls restrict access to physical spaces and resources, such as buildings, server rooms, and hardware devices. Examples include locks, badges, biometric scanners, and security guards.

Logical access controls restrict access to digital resources, such as files, databases, and applications. They are implemented through software and include measures like user accounts, passwords, and permissions.

Administrative access controls govern the management and configuration of access control systems themselves. They include processes for creating and managing user accounts, defining roles and permissions, and monitoring access logs.

ACCESS CONTROLS AND AUTHENTICATION

B. Authentication Models

Single-factor authentication relies on a single piece of information, such as a password, to verify a user's identity. While simple and widely used, single-factor authentication is vulnerable to various attacks, such as password guessing and phishing.

Two-factor authentication adds a second layer of security by requiring users to provide an additional piece of information, such as a one-time code sent to a mobile device, in addition to their password. 2FA significantly enhances security by making it harder for attackers to gain unauthorized access, even if they obtain a user's password.

Multi-factor authentication extends the concept of 2FA by requiring users to provide two or more pieces of evidence to verify their identity. This can include a combination of factors, such as something you know (a password), something you have (a smart card), and something you are (a fingerprint). MFA provides the highest level of authentication security by making it extremely difficult for attackers to compromise multiple factors.

ACCESS CONTROLS AND AUTHENTICATION

C. Authorization and Access Management

Role-based access control is a model that assigns permissions to users based on their roles or job functions within an organization. RBAC simplifies access management by grouping users with similar access needs into roles, rather than managing permissions individually for each user.

The principle of least privilege is a security best practice that states that users should be granted the minimum level of access necessary to perform their job functions. This helps minimize the potential impact of a compromised user account and reduces the risk of insider threats.

User account management involves the processes and procedures for creating, modifying, and deleting user accounts, as well as assigning and revoking permissions. Effective user account management includes practices like regular access reviews, prompt termination of unused accounts, and strong password policies.

BASIC CRYPTOGRAPHY CONCEPTS

A. Encryption and Decryption

Encryption is the process of converting plaintext into ciphertext to protect its confidentiality. Symmetric encryption uses a single key for both encryption and decryption, while asymmetric encryption uses a pair of keys (public and private) for these operations. Symmetric encryption is generally faster and more efficient, while asymmetric encryption provides additional security features, such as digital signatures.

Common symmetric encryption algorithms include Advanced Encryption Standard (AES) and Data Encryption Standard (DES), while common asymmetric algorithms include Rivest Shamir Adleman (RSA) and Elliptic Curve Cryptography (ECC). The choice of encryption algorithm depends on factors like security requirements, performance, and compatibility.

BASIC CRYPTOGRAPHY CONCEPTS

B. Hashing

Hash functions are mathematical algorithms that take an input of arbitrary size and produce an output of fixed size, called a hash or digest. Cryptographic hash functions have properties like the same input always produces the same output, it is infeasible to find an input that produces a given output, and it is infeasible to find two different inputs that produce the same output.

Secure hashing algorithms are cryptographic hash functions that are widely used for applications like password storage, data integrity verification, and digital signatures. Common secure hashing algorithms include SHA-256, SHA-3, and BLAKE2.

BASIC CRYPTOGRAPHY CONCEPTS

C. Digital Signatures and Certificates

Public key infrastructure is a framework that enables secure communication and authentication using asymmetric cryptography. PKI consists of components like certificate authorities (CAs), digital certificates, and certificate revocation lists (CRLs).

Certificate authorities are trusted entities that issue and manage digital certificates. Digital certificates are electronic documents that bind a public key to an identity, such as a person, organization, or device. Certificates are used for applications like secure email, web browsing (HTTPS), and code signing.

CHAPTER THREE

Master Security Operations

CHAPTER THREE
OBJECTIVES

After reading this chapter, the reader will be able to:

- Understand the importance of security operations in protecting an organization's data and systems
- Apply data security principles and best practices throughout the data handling process
- Classify data based on sensitivity levels and implement appropriate security controls
- Utilize logging and monitoring techniques to detect and respond to security incidents
- Understand the fundamentals of encryption and its role in protecting sensitive data
- Implement system hardening measures to reduce the attack surface and improve security posture
- Develop, implement, and enforce essential security policies, such as data handling, password, acceptable use, and change management
- Recognize the importance of security awareness training and its role in creating a strong security culture
- Identify and mitigate risks associated with insider threats and human error
- Continuously monitor and improve the organization's security posture through proactive measures and incident response planning

UNDERSTANDING DATA SECURITY

A. The Data Handling Process

Data is essential for modern organizations, and securing it requires a systematic approach that covers the entire data lifecycle. This process includes creating, storing, sharing, using, modifying, archiving, and ultimately destroying data. At each stage, best practices such as encryption, access controls, and secure backup and disposal methods must be applied to ensure the confidentiality, integrity, and availability of data.

B. Data Sensitivity Levels

Not all data is created equal, and understanding the different levels of data sensitivity is crucial for implementing appropriate security measures. Data can be classified into four main categories: high restricted, moderately restricted, low sensitivity, and unrestricted public data. Each level has specific implications for how data should be handled, stored, and shared. For example, highly restricted data, such as personal health information or financial records, requires the strongest security controls and most limited access.

UNDERSTANDING DATA SECURITY

C. Logging and Monitoring

Effective data security also requires robust logging and monitoring capabilities. Ingress monitoring tools, such as firewalls, gateways, and intrusion detection systems, help detect and prevent unauthorized access attempts. Egress monitoring, on the other hand, focuses on data leaving the organization through channels like email, file transfers, and web uploads. By keeping a close eye on both inbound and outbound data flows, organizations can quickly detect and respond to security incidents before they cause significant harm.

SYSTEM HARDENING ESSENTIALS

A. Configuration Management Procedures

System hardening is the process of securing a system by reducing its attack surface and vulnerabilities. A key aspect of system hardening is configuration management, which involves establishing and maintaining secure baselines for all systems and devices. Effective configuration management procedures include identification (inventorying all systems and their configurations), baselining (establishing secure default settings), change control (managing and approving configuration changes), verification (testing and validating changes), and auditing (regularly reviewing configurations for compliance and effectiveness).

B. Elements of Configuration Management

To implement configuration management effectively, organizations must focus on four key elements: inventory, baselines, updates, and patches. Maintaining an accurate inventory of all systems and their configurations is essential for knowing what needs to be secured. Baselines provide a secure starting point for each system type and ensure consistency across the environment. Regular updates and patching are critical for addressing known vulnerabilities and keeping systems protected against the latest threats.

SYSTEM HARDENING ESSENTIALS

C. Implementing System Hardening Measures

System hardening involves a variety of technical measures designed to reduce the attack surface and improve overall security. These measures include removing unnecessary services, applications, and protocols that could be exploited by attackers; configuring secure settings for operating systems, applications, and network devices; implementing strong access controls and authentication mechanisms; and regularly updating and patching systems to address known vulnerabilities. By taking a proactive approach to system hardening, organizations can significantly reduce their risk of compromise.

BEST PRACTICE SECURITY POLICIES

A. Essential Security Policies

Security policies are the foundation of an organization's cybersecurity program. They establish the rules, guidelines, and procedures that govern how systems and data are protected. Essential security policies include data handling, password, acceptable use, bring your own device (BYOD), privacy, and change management policies. Each policy serves a specific purpose, from ensuring the proper handling of sensitive data to defining acceptable use of company resources and managing the change control process.

B. Data Handling Policy Procedures

A data handling policy outlines the procedures for classifying, categorizing, labeling, storing, encrypting, backing up, and destroying data. It ensures that data is consistently managed throughout its lifecycle and that appropriate security controls are applied based on its sensitivity level. Best practices for implementing data handling policies include conducting regular data inventories, using standardized classification schemes, implementing strong encryption and access controls, and securely disposing of data when it is no longer needed.

BEST PRACTICE SECURITY POLICIES

A. Essential Security Policies

Security policies are the foundation of an organization's cybersecurity program. They establish the rules, guidelines, and procedures that govern how systems and data are protected. Essential security policies include data handling, password, acceptable use, bring your own device (BYOD), privacy, and change management policies. Each policy serves a specific purpose, from ensuring the proper handling of sensitive data to defining acceptable use of company resources and managing the change control process.

B. Data Handling Policy Procedures

A data handling policy outlines the procedures for classifying, categorizing, labeling, storing, encrypting, backing up, and destroying data. It ensures that data is consistently managed throughout its lifecycle and that appropriate security controls are applied based on its sensitivity level. Best practices for implementing data handling policies include conducting regular data inventories, using standardized classification schemes, implementing strong encryption and access controls, and securely disposing of data when it is no longer needed.

C. Password Policy Procedures

Password policies are designed to ensure that user accounts are protected by strong, complex passwords that are regularly updated. Key elements of a password policy include requirements for password length, complexity, and age, as well as guidelines for password creation, storage, and sharing. Enforcing strong password practices, such as using unique passwords for each account and enabling multi-factor authentication, can significantly reduce the risk of account compromise.

BEST PRACTICE SECURITY POLICIES

D. Acceptable Use Policy Procedures

An acceptable use policy (AUP) defines the appropriate use of an organization's systems, networks, and data. It covers topics such as data access, system access, data disclosure, password management, data retention, internet usage, and company device usage. The goal of an AUP is to ensure that users understand their responsibilities and the consequences of misuse. Organizations should educate users on the AUP and regularly enforce compliance through monitoring and disciplinary action.

E. BYOD Policy Considerations

Bring your own device (BYOD) policies have become increasingly important as more employees use personal devices for work purposes. A BYOD policy should define which devices are allowed (smartphones, tablets, laptops), what security requirements they must meet (encryption, password protection), and how they will be managed and supported. Organizations must balance the benefits of BYOD, such as increased flexibility and productivity, with the security risks posed by personal devices accessing corporate data and networks.

BEST PRACTICE SECURITY POLICIES

F. Privacy Policy and Regulations

Privacy policies are essential for protecting sensitive personal information, such as personally identifiable information (PII), electronic protected health information (ePHI), and financial data. These policies should define what types of information are collected, how they are used and shared, and what security measures are in place to protect them. Organizations must also ensure compliance with relevant privacy laws and regulations, such as the General Data Protection Regulation (GDPR) in the European Union and the Personal Information Protection and Electronic Documents Act (PIPEDA) in Canada.

G. Change Management Policy

A change management policy is designed to ensure that changes to an organization's systems and processes are properly planned, approved, implemented, and documented. The policy should define the change management process, including the roles and responsibilities of key stakeholders, the criteria for evaluating and prioritizing changes, and the procedures for testing and verifying changes before deployment. Effective change management is critical for maintaining the stability and security of an organization's IT environment.

SECURITY AWARENESS TRAINING

A. Types of Security Awareness Training

Security awareness training is an essential component of any cybersecurity program. It aims to educate users about the importance of security and their role in protecting an organization's assets. There are three main types of security awareness training: education (providing foundational knowledge), training (teaching specific skills and procedures), and awareness (reinforcing key messages and best practices). Each type plays a critical role in creating a culture of security and empowering users to be the first line of defense against cyber threats.

B. Countering Social Engineering Techniques

Social engineering is a common tactic used by attackers to manipulate users into divulging sensitive information or taking actions that compromise security. Techniques such as baiting (offering tempting but malicious content), phone phishing or vishing (using voice calls to trick users), pretexting (creating a false scenario to gain trust), quid pro quo (offering a service in exchange for information), tailgating (following someone into a secure area), and false flag (impersonating a trusted entity) are all designed to exploit human psychology and bypass technical controls.

To counter these threats, organizations must educate users on how to recognize and respond to social engineering attempts. This includes teaching them to be suspicious of unsolicited requests for information, to verify the identity of individuals before disclosing sensitive data, and to report any suspected social engineering attempts to security personnel.

SECURITY AWARENESS TRAINING

C. Implementing Effective Security Awareness Programs

Developing and implementing an effective security awareness program requires careful planning and execution. The first step is to assess the organization's training needs and define clear objectives for the program. This includes identifying the target audience, the key topics to be covered, and the desired outcomes.

Next, the program content must be developed in a way that is engaging, relevant, and memorable. This may involve using a variety of delivery methods, such as in-person training, e-learning modules, simulations, and gamification. The content should be tailored to the specific needs and roles of different user groups, such as executives, IT staff, and general employees.

Finally, the effectiveness of the security awareness program must be regularly measured and evaluated. This can be done through a combination of metrics, such as training completion rates, phishing simulation results, and user feedback surveys. By continuously monitoring and improving the program, organizations can ensure that it remains relevant and effective in the face of evolving cyber threats.

CHAPTER FOUR

Networking Concepts

CHAPTER FOUR OBJECTIVES

After reading this chapter, the reader will be able to:

- Understand the importance of network security in protecting an organization's assets and data
- Identify and differentiate between various types of computer networks and their applications
- Recognize the functions of essential network devices and their role in network communication
- Understand key networking terms, models, and protocols, such as the OSI and TCP/IP models
- Identify common network threats and attacks, such as DoS, DDoS, and Man-in-the-Middle attacks
- Utilize tools and techniques to detect and prevent network threats, such as IDS, IPS, and firewalls
- Understand the security implications of data center and cloud environments
- Implement network segmentation, VLANs, and other network design principles to enhance security
- Configure and manage essential network security controls, such as firewalls, IPS/IDS, and VPNs
- Stay informed about emerging network security trends and best practices to adapt to the evolving threat landscape

TYPES OF COMPUTER NETWORKS

A. Types of Computer Networks

Computer networks are classified based on their size, scope, and purpose.

Some of the most common types of networks include:

- Local Area Network (LAN): A network that connects devices within a limited area, such as an office or building. Example: A company's internal network connecting employees' computers, printers, and servers.
- Wide Area Network (WAN): A network that spans a large geographic area, connecting multiple LANs. Example: A corporation's network connecting branch offices across different countries.
- Wireless Local Area Network (WLAN): A LAN that uses wireless communication to connect devices. Example: A home network using Wi-Fi to connect laptops, smartphones, and smart home devices.
- Virtual Private Network (VPN): A secure, encrypted connection that allows remote users to access a private network over the internet. Example: An employee securely connecting to their company's network while working from a coffee shop.
- Enterprise Private Network (EPN): A private network that connects an organization's devices and resources across multiple locations. Example: A bank's network connecting ATMs, branch offices, and data centers.

TYPES OF COMPUTER NETWORKS

- Personal Area Network (PAN): A network that connects devices within a person's immediate area. Example: A smartwatch connected to a smartphone via Bluetooth.
- Metropolitan Area Network (MAN): A network that spans a city or metropolitan area. Example: A city's network connecting government offices, libraries, and public services.
- Storage Area Network (SAN): A dedicated high-speed network that provides access to consolidated, block-level data storage. Example: A network connecting an organization's servers to a centralized storage array.
- System Area Network (SAN): A high-performance network that connects computer systems and resources within a data center. Example: A network connecting servers, storage devices, and high-performance computing clusters.
- Passive Optical LAN (POLAN): A fiber-optic LAN that uses passive optical splitters to distribute signals to multiple devices. Example: A network connecting workstations and devices in a large office building using fiber-optic cables.

TYPES OF COMPUTER NETWORKS

B. Network Devices

Networks rely on various devices to facilitate communication and data transfer.

Some of the most essential network devices include:

- Hubs: Devices that connect multiple devices in a network and broadcast data to all connected devices. Example: A small office using a hub to connect computers and printers.
- Switches: Devices that connect multiple devices in a network and intelligently direct data to the intended recipient. Example: An organization using switches to segment its network and improve performance.
- Routers: Devices that connect multiple networks and forward data packets between them based on IP addresses. Example: A home router connecting a local network to the internet.
- Firewalls: Devices or software that monitor and control incoming and outgoing network traffic based on predetermined security rules. Example: A company using a firewall to block unauthorized access to its network.
- Servers: Computers that provide resources, services, or data to other devices on the network. Example: A web server hosting an organization's website.
- Printers: Devices that allow multiple users to print documents over a network. Example: An office printer connected to the local network for shared use.

TYPES OF COMPUTER NETWORKS

- Fax Machines: Devices that allow users to send and receive faxes over a network. Example: A multifunction printer with fax capabilities connected to a network.
- Gateways: Devices that connect networks using different protocols and translate data between them. Example: A VoIP gateway connecting a traditional phone system to an IP network.
- Repeaters: Devices that amplify or regenerate network signals to extend the transmission distance. Example: A repeater used to extend the range of a Wi-Fi network in a large warehouse.
- Bridges: Devices that connect two network segments and forward data between them based on MAC addresses. Example: A bridge connecting two separate LANs within an office.
- Modems: Devices that convert digital signals into analog signals for transmission over telephone lines, and vice versa. Example: A DSL modem connecting a home network to the internet.
- Access Points: Devices that allow wireless devices to connect to a wired network. Example: A Wi-Fi access point providing wireless connectivity in a conference room.

TYPES OF COMPUTER NETWORKS

C. Other Network Terms

Understanding key networking terms is essential for effectively communicating and working with networks.

Some important terms include:

- Packet: A unit of data that is transmitted over a network. Example: An email message broken down into multiple packets for transmission.
- Port: A logical endpoint for communication within a network. Example: Port 80 is commonly used for HTTP traffic.
- Protocol: A set of rules and standards that govern how devices communicate over a network. Example: The HTTP protocol is used for web communication.
- Ethernet: A family of wired network protocols that define how data is transmitted over a LAN. Example: Gigabit Ethernet is used in many modern networks.
- Wi-Fi: A family of wireless network protocols that define how data is transmitted over a WLAN. Example: The IEEE 802.11ac standard is used in many modern Wi-Fi networks.
- IP Address: A unique identifier assigned to each device on a network that uses the Internet Protocol (IP) for communication. Example: 192.168.1.1 is a common default IP address for home routers.
- MAC Address: A unique identifier assigned to a network interface card (NIC) by the manufacturer. Example: 00:11:22:33:44:55 is an example of a MAC address.

TYPES OF COMPUTER NETWORKS

D. Network Models

Network models provide a framework for understanding how data is transmitted over a network. The two most widely used network models are:

Open Systems Interconnection (OSI) Model is a conceptual model that divides network communication into seven layers, each responsible for a specific function.

1. Physical Layer:

- Defines the physical and electrical characteristics of the network hardware
- Specifies the transmission medium
- Establishes the relationship between a device and a transmission medium
- Examples: IEEE 802.11 (Wi-Fi)

2. Data Link Layer:

- Provides reliable data transfer between two devices on the same network
- Defines the format of data frames and handles error detection and correction
- Manages access to the physical medium using MAC (Media Access Control) addresses
- Examples: Ethernet (IEEE 802.3)

3. Network Layer:

- Responsible for routing packets between different networks
- Provides logical addressing (IP addresses) and path determination
- Handles network congestion and quality of service
- Examples: IP (Internet Protocol)

TYPES OF COMPUTER NETWORKS

4. Transport Layer:

- Ensures reliable end-to-end data delivery between applications
- Segments data into smaller units and reassembles them at the destination
- Provides flow control, error recovery, and congestion control
- Examples: TCP (Transmission Control Protocol), UDP (User Datagram Protocol)

5. Session Layer:

- Establishes, manages, and terminates sessions between applications
- Provides synchronization and checkpointing mechanisms for long-running transactions
- Examples: RPC (Remote Procedure Call), NetBIOS, PPTP (Point-to-Point Tunneling Protocol)

6. Presentation Layer:

- Handles data representation and encryption
- Converts data between different formats
- Compresses data to reduce transmission time
- Examples: SSL (Secure Sockets Layer), TLS (Transport Layer Security), MIME (Multipurpose Internet Mail Extensions)

7. Application Layer:

- Provides services directly to the end-user applications
- Defines protocols for specific applications, such as email, file transfer, and web browsing
- Examples: HTTP (Hypertext Transfer Protocol), FTP (File Transfer Protocol), SMTP (Simple Mail Transfer Protocol)

TYPES OF COMPUTER NETWORKS

Transmission Control Protocol/Internet Protocol (TCP/IP) Model is a practical model that divides network communication into four layers, and is the foundation of the internet.

1. Network Interface Layer :

- Combines the functionalities of the Physical and Data Link layers of the OSI model
- Defines how data is physically transmitted over the network medium

2. Internet Layer:

- Equivalent to the Network layer of the OSI model
- Responsible for routing packets between networks using IP addresses
- Provides connectionless, best-effort delivery of packets

3. Transport Layer:

- Equivalent to the Transport layer of the OSI model
- Provides end-to-end data delivery services
- Offers connection-oriented (TCP) and connectionless (UDP) protocols

4. Application Layer:

- Combines the functionalities of the Session, Presentation, and Application layers of the OSI model
- Defines protocols and services used by end-user applications

TYPES OF COMPUTER NETWORKS

E. IPv4 vs. IPv6

Internet Protocol (IP) is the primary protocol used for communication over the internet. There are two versions of IP currently in use:

- IPv4: The fourth version of the Internet Protocol, which uses 32-bit addresses and can support up to 4.3 billion unique addresses. Example: 192.0.2.1 is an IPv4 address.
- IPv6: The sixth version of the Internet Protocol, which uses 128-bit addresses and can support a virtually unlimited number of unique addresses. Example: 2001:0db8:85a3:0000:0000:8a2e:0370:7334 is an IPv6 address.

NETWORK THREATS AND ATTACKS

A. Types of Network Attacks

Networks face a wide range of attacks designed to compromise the confidentiality, integrity, or availability of data and resources.

Some common types of network attacks include:

- Denial of Service (DoS): An attack that aims to make a network resource unavailable to its intended users by overwhelming it with traffic or requests.
- Distributed Denial of Service (DDoS): A DoS attack that uses multiple compromised systems to flood the target with traffic or requests.
- Fragment Attack: An attack that exploits the fragmentation of IP packets to evade detection or bypass security controls.
- Oversized Packet Attack: An attack that sends packets larger than the maximum allowed size to cause a buffer overflow or crash on the target system.
- Spoofing: An attack that involves disguising the source of network traffic to impersonate a trusted entity or gain unauthorized access.
- Man-in-the-Middle (MitM): An attack that intercepts and potentially alters communication between two parties without their knowledge.
- SQL Injection: An attack that exploits vulnerabilities in web applications to insert malicious SQL code into database queries.
- Cross-Site Scripting (XSS): An attack that injects malicious scripts into trusted websites to steal user data or perform unauthorized actions.
- Privilege Escalation: An attack that exploits vulnerabilities or misconfigurations to gain elevated access or permissions on a system.
- Insider Threat: A security risk that originates from within the organization, such as a malicious or negligent employee.

NETWORK THREATS AND ATTACKS

B. Types of Networking Threats

Networks are also susceptible to various threats that can compromise security. Some common networking threats include:

Spoofing: Disguising the source of network traffic to impersonate a trusted entity or gain unauthorized access. Example: An attacker using IP spoofing to bypass access controls.

- DoS/DDoS: Overwhelming a network resource with traffic or requests to make it unavailable to its intended users. Example: An attacker using a botnet to launch a DDoS attack against a website.
- Virus: A type of malware that replicates itself and spreads to other systems by attaching itself to legitimate files or programs. Example: A computer virus that spreads via infected email attachments.
- Worm: A type of malware that replicates itself and spreads to other systems over a network without requiring human interaction. Example: The WannaCry ransomware worm that spread rapidly across networks in 2017.
- Trojan: A type of malware that disguises itself as a legitimate program to trick users into installing it, and then performs malicious actions. Example: A trojan horse that poses as a free game but secretly steals user data.

NETWORK THREATS AND ATTACKS

- Rootkit: A type of malware designed to hide its presence and grant an attacker persistent access to a compromised system. Example: A kernel-level rootkit that modifies the operating system to evade detection.
- Adware: Software that displays unwanted advertisements to users, often bundled with free applications. Example: A free mobile game that displays intrusive pop-up ads.
- Malware: A broad term encompassing any software designed to harm, disrupt, or gain unauthorized access to a computer system. Example: Ransomware that encrypts a victim's files and demands payment for the decryption key.
- On-Path Attack: An attack where the attacker has the ability to intercept and modify network traffic between two communicating parties. Example: An attacker using a compromised network device to intercept and modify data in transit.
- Side-Channel Attack: An attack that exploits information leakage from a system's physical implementation to gain unauthorized access or sensitive data. Example: An attacker using power analysis to extract cryptographic keys from a smart card.
- Phishing: A social engineering attack that attempts to trick users into revealing sensitive information or installing malware. Example: An attacker sending fake emails purporting to be from a bank, asking users to verify their login credentials.

NETWORK THREATS AND ATTACKS

C. Ports and Protocols

Ports and protocols are essential components of network communication.

Some commonly used ports and protocols include:

- Port 80 (HTTP): Used for unencrypted web traffic. Example: Visiting a website that does not use HTTPS.
- Port 443 (HTTPS): Used for encrypted web traffic. Example: Logging into an online banking platform.
- Port 22 (SSH): Used for secure remote access to a system. Example: Administering a remote server using SSH.
- Port 21 (FTP): Used for transferring files between systems. Example: Uploading a website's files to a web server.
- Port 25 (SMTP): Used for sending email messages. Example: Sending an email using a mail client.
- Port 53 (DNS): Used for resolving domain names to IP addresses. Example: Accessing a website by its domain name.
- Port 3389 (RDP): Used for remote desktop access to a Windows system. Example: Remotely accessing a work computer from home.

NETWORK THREATS AND ATTACKS

D. Identifying Threats

Several tools and techniques are used to identify network threats such as:

- Intrusion Detection Systems (IDS): Tools that monitor network traffic for suspicious activities and alert administrators of potential threats. Example: Snort, an open-source IDS that uses rules to detect network intrusions.
- Network Intrusion Detection Systems (NIDS): IDS that monitor network traffic at the network level. Example: Suricata, a high-performance NIDS that can detect a wide range of network threats.
- Host Intrusion Detection Systems (HIDS): IDS that monitor activity on individual hosts or devices. Example: OSSEC, an open-source HIDS that performs log analysis, file integrity checking, and rootkit detection.
- Security Information and Event Management (SIEM): Tools that collect and analyze log data from various sources to identify security incidents and threats. Example: Splunk, a popular SIEM platform that provides real-time monitoring, alerting, and analytics.

NETWORK THREATS AND ATTACKS

E. Preventing Threats

Several tools and techniques are used to prevent network threats, including:

- Antivirus Software: Tools that detect and remove malware from systems. Example: Norton AntiVirus, a popular antivirus solution for home and business users.
- Vulnerability Scans: Automated tools that scan systems and networks for known vulnerabilities and misconfigurations. Example: Nessus, a comprehensive vulnerability scanner used by many organizations.
- Firewalls: Devices or software that monitor and control incoming and outgoing network traffic based on predetermined security rules. Example: pfSense, an open-source firewall and router platform.
- Intrusion Prevention Systems (IPS): Tools that monitor network traffic and actively block detected threats. Example: Cisco Next-Generation Intrusion Prevention System, a network security appliance that combines IPS, advanced malware protection, and application visibility and control.
- Network Intrusion Prevention Systems (NIPS): IPS that operate at the network level. Example: Trend Micro TippingPoint, a NIPS that provides real-time threat prevention and advanced threat protection.
- Host Intrusion Prevention Systems (HIPS): IPS that operate at the host or device level. Example: McAfee Host Intrusion Prevention for Server, a HIPS solution that protects servers from advanced threats and unauthorized changes.

DATA CENTER AND CLOUD CONCEPTS

A. Requirements for a Data Center

Data centers are facilities that house an organization's critical IT infrastructure.

Some key requirements for data centers include:

- Power: Reliable and redundant power supply to ensure continuous operation. Example: Uninterruptible Power Supply (UPS) systems and backup generators.
- HVAC: Adequate cooling and humidity control to maintain optimal operating conditions for equipment. Example: Precision air conditioning units and hot aisle/cold aisle containment.
- Fire Suppression: Systems to detect and suppress fires to protect equipment and data. Example: Clean agent fire suppression systems, such as FM-200 or Novec 1230.
- Redundancy: Duplicate equipment and infrastructure to minimize downtime in case of failures. Example: Redundant network switches, routers, and storage arrays.
- Memorandum of Understanding/Agreement (MOU/MOA): Agreements between organizations to define roles, responsibilities, and expectations for shared data center resources. Example: An MOU between two companies sharing a colocation data center.

DATA CENTER AND CLOUD CONCEPTS

B. Cloud Service Models

Cloud computing offers various service models to meet different organizational needs.

The three main cloud service models are:

- Software as a Service (SaaS): Applications hosted by a provider and accessed over the internet. Example: Microsoft Office 365, a suite of productivity applications delivered via the cloud.
- Infrastructure as a Service (IaaS): Virtualized computing resources, such as servers, storage, and networks, provisioned and managed over the internet. Example: Amazon Web Services (AWS) Elastic Compute Cloud (EC2), which provides resizable compute capacity in the cloud.
- Platform as a Service (PaaS): A platform for developing, running, and managing applications without the complexity of building and maintaining the underlying infrastructure. Example: Google App Engine, a PaaS offering that allows developers to build and host web applications on Google's infrastructure.

DATA CENTER AND CLOUD CONCEPTS

C. Cloud Deployment Models

In addition to the service models, there are different ways a cloud environment can be deployed:

- Public cloud: IT resources are provisioned via the public internet from a third-party provider's data centers and shared across multiple tenants. Offers the greatest scalability and cost-efficiency. Examples include AWS, Azure, and Google Cloud.
- Private cloud: Cloud infrastructure dedicated to a single organization, either on-premises or hosted by a provider. Provides the most control and security. Examples include VMware vSphere, Microsoft Azure Stack, and OpenStack.
- Hybrid cloud: Combines public and private cloud resources, allowing workloads to move between them. Balances scalability and control. An example might be running customer-facing apps in public cloud while keeping sensitive back-end databases in private cloud.
- Multi-cloud: Uses multiple public cloud providers to avoid vendor lock-in or leverage best-of-breed services. Requires careful management and integration. An example could be using AWS for compute, Azure for machine learning, and Google for big data analytics.

DATA CENTER AND CLOUD CONCEPTS

D. Network Design Terminology

When architecting data center and cloud networks, it's important to understand key concepts such as:

- Availability: The proportion of time a network is functioning normally.
- Scalability: The ability of a network to grow and handle increased demand.
- Redundancy: Having multiple instances of critical components to maintain operations if one fails.
- Throughput: The amount of data that can transferred across a network per unit of time, typically measured in Gbps for data center networks.
- Latency: The delay in data transmission over a network, measured in milliseconds.
- Jitter: The variation in latency over time, which can disrupt real-time applications like VoIP and video conferencing.
- Quality of Service: Mechanisms for prioritizing certain traffic flows over a network.

NETWORK SECURITY CONTROLS

A. Firewalls

Firewalls are a critical first line of defense for any network. They monitor and filter traffic between networks based on an established security policy. Firewalls come in different forms, including:

- Network firewalls: Hardware or software that filters traffic between network segments. An example is Cisco Adaptive Security Appliance.
- Host-based firewalls: Software running on individual servers or endpoints, such as Windows Defender Firewall or iptables on Linux.
- Next-generation firewalls (NGFWs): Firewalls with advanced features like application awareness, intrusion prevention, and user identity management. Examples include Palo Alto Networks and Fortinet FortiGate.

B. Intrusion Prevention Systems (IPS) and Intrusion Detection Systems (IDS)

IDS/IPS solutions detect and block network threats in real-time. Key differences:

- IDS is passive, monitoring network traffic and generating alerts without blocking threats. Examples include Snort and Security Onion.
- IPS is active, monitoring traffic and automatically blocking detected threats. Examples include McAfee Network Security Platform and Trend Micro TippingPoint.

IDS/IPS use techniques like signature matching, anomaly detection, and reputation analysis to spot threats. They should be deployed at network perimeters and key internal segments.

NETWORK SECURITY CONTROLS

C. Proxies and Web Filtering

Secure web gateways protect users and networks from internet-based threats and enforce acceptable use policies. Two key technologies:

- Proxy servers act as an intermediary between users and the internet, controlling access and caching content. Proxies can filter URLs, scan for malware, and decrypt SSL traffic for inspection. Examples include Blue Coat ProxySG and Squid.
- Web filters restrict access to risky sites and content based on categories like violence, hate speech, porn, and gambling. Filters use URL databases and content analysis to categorize sites. Examples include Barracuda Web Filter and Cisco Umbrella.

D. Virtual Private Networks (VPNs)

VPNs create an encrypted tunnel for securely connecting remote users and sites over untrusted networks like the internet. Benefits of VPNs include:

- Confidentiality: Encryption prevents eavesdropping of sensitive data
- Authentication: Only authorized users can access VPN endpoints
- Integrity: Hashing ensures data is not altered in transit

Common VPN protocols include IPsec (Cisco AnyConnect) and SSL/TLS (OpenVPN).

Software-defined wide area network solutions like Cisco Viptela can automatically route traffic across multiple VPN links for optimal performance.

CHAPTER FIVE

Cyber Threat Analysis

CHAPTER FIVE OBJECTIVES

After reading this chapter, the reader will be able to:

- Understand the importance of cyber threat analysis in protecting an organization's assets and data
- Identify and classify various types of cyber threats, such as malware, social engineering, and network-based attacks
- Recognize the characteristics and impact of Advanced Persistent Threats
- Understand the motivations behind different threat actors, such as financial gain, espionage, and hacktivism
- Analyze the stages of the Cyber Kill Chain and Targeted Attack Lifecycle to identify opportunities for detection and mitigation
- Apply lessons learned from real-world attack scenarios and case studies to improve an organization's security posture
- Understand the role of ethical hacking, penetration testing, and red teaming in assessing an organization's security defenses
- Utilize threat intelligence and anomaly detection techniques to proactively search for hidden threats
- Develop a security mindset that involves thinking like an attacker and adopting a proactive approach to security
- Foster a culture of security awareness and encourage responsible disclosure and reporting of potential security issues

TYPES OF CYBER THREATS

A. Malware

Malware, short for malicious software, is any program designed to harm, disrupt, or gain unauthorized access to a computer system.

Common types of malware include:

- Viruses: Self-replicating programs that attach themselves to legitimate files and spread from one system to another.
- Worms: Stand-alone malware that propagates through networks without requiring human interaction.
- Trojans: Malware disguised as legitimate software, tricking users into installing it.
- Ransomware: Malware that encrypts a victim's files and demands a ransom payment for the decryption key.

TYPES OF CYBER THREATS

B. Social Engineering

Social engineering involves manipulating people into divulging sensitive information or performing actions that compromise security.

Common social engineering techniques include:

- Phishing: Sending fraudulent emails that appear to be from a trustworthy source to trick recipients into revealing sensitive information or clicking on malicious links. Example: An email claiming to be from a bank, asking users to verify their account details.
- Spear phishing: A targeted form of phishing that uses personalized information to make the attack more convincing. Example: An email addressed to a specific employee, referencing a recent project they worked on.
- Baiting: Exploiting human curiosity or greed by offering free gifts or downloads that contain malware. Example: A USB drive left in a public place, labeled with an enticing title.
- Pretexting: Creating a fabricated scenario to gain a victim's trust and extract sensitive information. Example: An attacker posing as an IT support technician, asking for login credentials to resolve a fictional issue.

TYPES OF CYBER THREATS

C. Network-based Threats

Network-based threats target vulnerabilities in an organization's network infrastructure to compromise systems and data.

Examples include:

- Denial of Service attacks: Overwhelming a network or system with traffic to make it unavailable to users.
- Distributed Denial of Service attacks: A DoS attack that uses multiple compromised systems to amplify its impact.
- Man-in-the-Middle attacks: Intercepting communication between two parties to eavesdrop or alter the data being transmitted.
- SQL injection: Exploiting vulnerabilities in web applications to insert malicious SQL statements and access or manipulate database content.

TYPES OF CYBER THREATS

D. Advanced Persistent Threats (APTs)

APTs are sophisticated, long-term attacks that target specific organizations to steal sensitive data or disrupt operations.

Key characteristics of APTs include:

- Stealthy and persistent: APTs use advanced techniques to evade detection and maintain access to compromised systems over an extended period.
- Targeted and customized: APTs are tailored to specific organizations and often involve extensive planning and research.

Examples of notable APT attacks:

- Operation Aurora (2009): A series of cyber attacks targeting major companies, including Google and Adobe, to steal intellectual property and gain access to activist email accounts.
- Stuxnet (2010): A highly sophisticated malware that targeted Iranian nuclear facilities, causing significant damage to centrifuges used in uranium enrichment.

UNDERSTANDING THREAT ACTOR MOTIVATIONS

To effectively analyze and mitigate cyber threats, it's essential to understand the motivations behind them. Common threat actor motivations include:

A. Financial Gain

- Cybercriminals and organized crime groups: These threat actors seek to monetize their attacks through various means, such as stealing financial data, selling stolen information on the dark web, or extorting victims.
- Ransomware attacks and extortion: Ransomware has become a lucrative business model for cybercriminals, with victims often paying significant sums to regain access to their data.

B. Espionage

- Nation-state sponsored attacks: Governments engage in cyber espionage to gain strategic, economic, or military advantages over rival nations. Example: The US Office of Personnel Management data breach in 2015, attributed to Chinese state-sponsored hackers.
- Industrial espionage and intellectual property theft: Competitors may use cyber attacks to steal trade secrets and gain an unfair market advantage.

UNDERSTANDING THREAT ACTOR MOTIVATIONS

C. Hacktivism

- Hacktivist groups, such as Anonymous, launch attacks to promote political or social causes, expose perceived wrongdoings, or express dissent.
- Hacktivists may target organizations to expose sensitive information or support whistleblowers.

D. Insider Threats

- Insiders with legitimate access to systems and data may abuse their privileges to cause harm or steal information, often motivated by revenge or financial gain.
- Not all insider threats are malicious; employees may accidentally expose data or fall victim to social engineering attacks due to lack of awareness or training.

CYBER KILL CHAIN

The Cyber Kill Chain is a framework developed by Lockheed Martin that describes the stages of a targeted cyber attack. Understanding this lifecycle is crucial for identifying opportunities to detect, disrupt, and mitigate attacks.

A. Reconnaissance

- Attackers collect publicly available information about the target organization, such as employee names, email addresses, and social media profiles.
- Attackers use tools to scan networks and systems for vulnerabilities and gather information about the target's infrastructure.

B. Weaponization

- Attackers create or modify malware to exploit specific vulnerabilities and evade detection by security tools.
- Attackers develop exploits to take advantage of identified vulnerabilities and create payloads to deliver malware or establish a foothold in the target environment.

C. Delivery

- Attackers use crafted emails and social engineering techniques to trick users into opening malicious attachments or clicking on links that download malware.
- Attackers compromise websites frequently used by the target organization's employees to spread malware.

CYBER KILL CHAIN

D. Exploitation

- Attackers use exploits to take advantage of vulnerabilities in systems, applications, or networks to gain unauthorized access.
- Once a system is compromised, attackers establish a persistent presence to maintain access and pivot to other systems.

E. Installation

- Attackers use techniques like modifying registry keys, creating scheduled tasks, or installing backdoors to ensure continued access to the compromised system.
- Attackers move laterally across the network, exploiting vulnerabilities and misconfigurations to gain higher levels of access and compromise additional systems.

F. Command and Control (C2)

- Attackers establish secure communication channels to control compromised systems, issue commands, and exfiltrate data.
- Attackers use C2 channels to remotely access compromised systems, steal sensitive data, and cover their tracks.

G. Actions on Objectives

- Attackers carry out their ultimate objectives, such as data theft, sabotage, or establishing a long-term presence for future attacks.
- Attackers hide their activities, delete logs, and ensure they can maintain access to the compromised environment for future operations.

REAL WORLD ATTACK SCENARIOS

Examining real-world cyber attacks provides valuable insights into threat actor tactics, techniques, and procedures, as well as lessons learned for improving cybersecurity posture.

A. WannaCry Ransomware Attack (2017)

WannaCry exploited a vulnerability in the Windows SMB protocol to spread rapidly across networks, encrypting files and demanding bitcoin payments for decryption. The attack affected over 200,000 computers in 150 countries, causing significant disruption to businesses and public services.

Lessons learned and takeaways:

- Keep systems and software up to date with the latest security patches.
- Implement a robust backup and recovery strategy to mitigate the impact of ransomware attacks.
- Educate employees about the risks of phishing emails and suspicious attachments.

REAL WORLD ATTACK SCENARIOS

B. SolarWinds Supply Chain Attack (2020)

Attackers compromised the software update mechanism of SolarWinds' Orion IT management platform, distributing a backdoor to thousands of customers, including government agencies and Fortune 500 companies. The attack went undetected for months, allowing the attackers to conduct espionage and steal sensitive data.

Lessons learned and takeaways:

- Implement rigorous security controls and monitoring for software development and update processes.
- Use a risk-based approach to assess and manage third-party vendor security.
- Adopt a zero-trust security model to minimize the impact of breaches.

OFFENSIVE SECURITY CONCEPTS

Offensive security involves proactively identifying and exploiting vulnerabilities in systems and networks to assess and improve an organization's security posture.

A. Ethical Hacking and Penetration Testing

Ethical hacking involves using the same techniques as malicious hackers to identify vulnerabilities and assess the effectiveness of an organization's security controls. Penetration testing is a form of ethical hacking that simulates real-world attacks to evaluate the security of systems and networks.

Ethical hacking and penetration testing must be conducted with the explicit permission of the organization and within the scope of a well-defined engagement. Ethical hackers must adhere to strict legal and ethical guidelines, such as the EC-Council Code of Ethics.

B. Red Teaming

Red teaming involves a group of ethical hackers simulating the tactics, techniques, and procedures of real-world threat actors to assess an organization's detection and response capabilities. Red team engagements are designed to be as realistic as possible, often involving social engineering, physical access attempts, and advanced persistent threat scenarios.

Red team exercises help organizations identify gaps in their security posture, test incident response plans, and improve their ability to detect and respond to advanced threats.

OFFENSIVE SECURITY CONCEPTS

C. Threat Hunting

Threat hunting is the practice of proactively searching for signs of compromise or malicious activity that have evaded traditional security controls. Threat hunters use a combination of automated tools, data analytics, and manual investigation techniques to uncover hidden threats.

Threat hunting relies on threat intelligence, which provides insights into the tactics, techniques, and procedures used by threat actors. Anomaly detection techniques, such as machine learning and behavioral analysis, help identify unusual patterns and activities that may indicate the presence of a threat.

DEVELOPING A SECURITY MINDSET

To effectively analyze and mitigate cyber threats, cybersecurity professionals must develop a security mindset that involves thinking like an attacker, adopting a proactive approach to security, and fostering a culture of security awareness.

A. Thinking like an attacker

To anticipate and defend against cyber threats, it's essential to understand how attackers operate. This involves studying real-world attacks, keeping up with the latest threat intelligence, and participating in offensive security exercises like capture the flag competitions.

By thinking like an attacker, cybersecurity professionals can proactively identify potential entry points and weaknesses in their organization's defenses. This mindset helps prioritize security efforts and allocate resources effectively.

B. Adopting a proactive security approach

A proactive security approach involves continuously monitoring systems and networks for signs of compromise or malicious activity. This includes using security information and event management tools, intrusion detection and prevention systems, and endpoint detection and response solutions.

Proactive security also involves developing and regularly testing incident response plans to ensure that the organization can quickly and effectively respond to security incidents. This includes conducting tabletop exercises and simulations to identify gaps and improve response capabilities.

DEVELOPING A SECURITY MINDSET

C. Fostering a culture of security awareness

A strong security culture starts with educating employees about the importance of cybersecurity and their role in protecting the organization. This includes regular training on topics like identifying phishing emails, creating strong passwords, and handling sensitive data securely.

Organizations should foster an environment where employees feel comfortable reporting potential security issues or suspicious activities. This includes establishing clear reporting channels and promoting a culture of trust and transparency.

CHAPTER SIX

Leveraging Linux and Python

CHAPTER SIX OBJECTIVES

After reading this chapter, the reader will be able to:

- Understand the importance of Linux and Python in the field of cybersecurity.
- Navigate the Linux file system, manage files and directories, and use essential Linux commands for cybersecurity tasks.
- Manage Linux packages, users, groups, and processes.
- Write basic Bash scripts to automate cybersecurity tasks, such as log analysis and system hardening.
- Set up a Python development environment and understand basic Python syntax and concepts.
- Work with files and directories, handle errors, and use important Python libraries for cybersecurity.
- Apply Python programming to various cybersecurity tasks, including network scanning, web scraping, encryption, log analysis, malware analysis, and developing custom security tools.

LINUX FUNDAMENTALS

A. Understanding the Linux File System

To navigate and utilize Linux effectively, it is crucial to understand its file system structure. The Linux file system follows a hierarchical directory structure, with the root directory (/) serving as the top-level directory. Key directories include:

- /bin: Essential command binaries
- /etc: System configuration files
- /home: User home directories
- /var: Variable files (logs, databases)

File permissions and ownership play a vital role in maintaining the security of a Linux system. Each file and directory has associated permissions that determine the level of access granted to users and groups. Understanding and properly managing file permissions is essential for preventing unauthorized access and ensuring the integrity of system resources.

LINUX FUNDAMENTALS

B. Essential Linux Commands for Cybersecurity

Linux provides a rich set of command-line tools that are indispensable for cybersecurity professionals. Here are some essential commands to master:

System Information Commands:

- uname: Displays system information
- whoami: Shows the current user
- id: Displays user and group information

File and Directory Manipulation:

- ls: Lists directory contents
- cp: Copies files and directories
- mv: Moves or renames files and directories
- rm: Removes files and directories
- mkdir: Creates directories

Text Processing:

- grep: Searches for patterns in files
- sed: Stream editor for text manipulation
- awk: Powerful text processing tool

Network-Related Commands:

- ifconfig: Configures network interfaces
- netstat: Displays network connections and statistics
- ss: Socket statistics tool

LINUX FUNDAMENTALS

C. Package Management

Linux distributions provide package management systems to simplify software installation and updates. The two most common package managers are:

- APT (Advanced Package Tool): Used in Debian-based systems like Ubuntu
-
- YUM (Yellowdog Updater Modified): Used in Red Hat-based systems like CentOS

Familiarizing yourself with package management commands will enable you to install, update, and remove software packages efficiently.

D. User and Group Management

Linux is a multi-user operating system, and effective user and group management is crucial for maintaining security. Key concepts include creating and managing user accounts, assigning appropriate permissions, and configuring user roles and privileges.

E. Process Management and Monitoring

Understanding how to manage and monitor processes is essential for identifying and responding to potential security threats. Commands like ps, top, and htop allow you to view running processes, monitor system resource usage, and terminate suspicious or malicious processes.

INTRODUCTION TO BASH SCRIPTING

Bash (Bourne-Again Shell) is the default shell in most Linux distributions, and mastering Bash scripting is a valuable skill for automating repetitive tasks and creating custom tools. Here are the key concepts to grasp:

A. Basic Script Structure and Execution

A Bash script is a plain text file containing a series of commands. It begins with a shebang #!/bin/bash to specify the interpreter. Scripts are executed using the bash command or by making the script file executable with the chmod command.

B. Variables and Data Types

Bash supports variables to store and manipulate data. Variables are declared using the syntax variable_name=value and accessed using the $ symbol $variable_name. Bash has various data types, including strings, integers, and arrays.

INTRODUCTION TO BASH SCRIPTING

C. Control Structures

Control structures allow you to control the flow of execution in a Bash script. Key control structures include:

- if-else statements for conditional execution
- for and while loops for iteration

D. Functions and Modularity

Functions enable you to break down your script into reusable and modular pieces of code. They are defined using the function keyword followed by the function name and a set of parentheses. Functions can accept arguments and return values.

E. Command Substitution and Piping

Command substitution allows you to capture the output of a command and assign it to a variable using the $() syntax. Piping (|) enables you to pass the output of one command as input to another command, creating powerful command chains.

INTRODUCTION TO BASH SCRIPTING

F. Error Handling and Debugging

Proper error handling and debugging techniques are essential for creating robust Bash scripts. The exit command is used to terminate a script with a specific exit status. The set -x command enables debugging mode, displaying each command as it is executed.

G. Practical Examples of Bash Scripts for Cybersecurity Tasks

- Log Analysis Script: A Bash script that parses log files, extracts relevant information, and generates a report of suspicious activities.
- Automated System Hardening Script: A script that automates the process of applying security best practices and hardening a Linux system, such as configuring firewall rules, disabling unnecessary services, and setting secure file permissions.

GETTING STARTED WITH PYTHON

Python is a high-level, versatile programming language widely used in cybersecurity for automating tasks, developing tools, and performing data analysis.

A. Python Installation and Environment Setup

Python is available for various operating systems, including Linux, macOS, and Windows. It is recommended to use Python 3.x, as it is the latest stable version. You can download Python from the official Python website (https://www.python.org) and follow the installation instructions specific to your operating system.

After installing Python, it's a good practice to set up a virtual environment. Virtual environments allow you to create isolated Python environments for different projects, ensuring that dependencies and packages are managed separately. You can create a virtual environment using the venv module in Python.

GETTING STARTED WITH PYTHON

B. Python Syntax and Basic Concepts

Python has a clean and readable syntax, making it beginner-friendly. Here are some basic concepts to understand:

- Python is a dynamically-typed language, meaning you don't need to explicitly declare variable types. Python supports various data types, including strings (str), integers (int), floating-point numbers (float), booleans (bool), lists (list), tuples (tuple), and dictionaries (dict).
- Python provides control structures for conditional execution and looping. The if-else statement is used for conditional execution, while for and while loops are used for iteration.
- Functions are reusable blocks of code that perform specific tasks. They are defined using the def keyword, followed by the function name and a set of parentheses. Python also supports modules, which are files containing Python definitions and statements. Modules allow you to organize your code into logical units and reuse functionality across different scripts.

C. Working with Files and Directories in Python

Python provides built-in functions and modules for working with files and directories. The open() function is used to open files for reading or writing, while the os module provides functions for interacting with the operating system, such as navigating directories, creating folders, and manipulating file paths.

GETTING STARTED WITH PYTHON

D. Error Handling and Exceptions

Error handling is an essential aspect of writing robust Python code. Python uses exceptions to handle errors and exceptional conditions. The try-except block is used to catch and handle exceptions gracefully. It allows you to specify the code that may raise an exception within the try block and define how to handle specific exceptions in the corresponding except blocks.

E. Introduction to Important Python Libraries for Cybersecurity

Python has a rich ecosystem of libraries and frameworks that are particularly useful for cybersecurity tasks. Here are a few essential libraries to explore:

- os and sys: These built-in modules provide functions for interacting with the operating system, such as executing system commands, accessing environment variables, and manipulating file paths.
- requests: The requests library simplifies making HTTP requests from Python. It allows you to send GET, POST, and other types of requests to web servers, handle authentication, and retrieve response data.
- socket: The socket module enables low-level network programming in Python. It provides functions for creating socket connections, sending and receiving data over the network, and implementing network protocols.

PYTHON FOR CYBERSECURITY TASKS

A. Network Scanning and Enumeration

Python's extensive network programming capabilities make it an excellent choice for network scanning and enumeration tasks.

- Scapy is a powerful Python library for packet manipulation and network scanning. It allows you to craft, send, sniff, and dissect network packets, making it useful for tasks like network mapping, vulnerability assessment, and intrusion detection.
- With Python, you can create a basic port scanner to identify open ports on a target system. By leveraging the socket module, you can establish connections to specific ports and determine their status (open, closed, or filtered).

B. Web Scraping and Reconnaissance

Python's web scraping capabilities enable you to extract valuable information from websites for reconnaissance and intelligence gathering purposes.

- BeautifulSoup is a popular Python library for parsing HTML and XML documents. It provides a convenient way to navigate and search the parsed data, making it ideal for web scraping tasks.
- Python can be used to automate Open-Source Intelligence tasks, such as gathering information from public sources, social media platforms, and online databases. By leveraging libraries like requests and beautifulsoup, you can create scripts to collect and analyze publicly available data.

PYTHON FOR CYBERSECURITY TASKS

C. Encryption and Decryption

Python provides libraries for implementing encryption and decryption algorithms, allowing you to secure sensitive data and communications.

1. The cryptography library is a comprehensive Python package for cryptographic operations. It supports various encryption algorithms, such as symmetric encryption (AES), asymmetric encryption (RSA), and hashing functions (SHA-256).
2. Python allows you to implement basic encryption algorithms from scratch, helping you understand the underlying concepts. You can create scripts to encrypt and decrypt data using algorithms like Caesar cipher, substitution ciphers, or more advanced techniques like public-key cryptography.

D. Log Analysis and Intrusion Detection

Python's text processing capabilities and libraries make it well-suited for log analysis and intrusion detection tasks.

1. Python provides powerful text processing capabilities through libraries like `re` (regular expressions) and `pandas` (data manipulation and analysis). You can create scripts to parse log files, extract relevant information, and perform analysis to identify anomalies or suspicious activities.

2. By combining log analysis techniques with machine learning algorithms, you can develop a basic intrusion detection system using Python. Libraries like `scikit-learn` offer a wide range of machine learning algorithms that can be trained on log data to detect patterns and anomalies indicative of potential intrusions.

PYTHON FOR CYBERSECURITY TASKS

E. Malware Analysis

Python is extensively used in malware analysis, both for static analysis and dynamic analysis tasks.

- Static analysis involves examining malware samples without executing them. Python libraries like pefile and capstone enable you to parse and analyze executable files, extract metadata, and disassemble code for further analysis.
- Dynamic analysis involves executing malware samples in a controlled environment to observe their behavior. Python can automate tasks like setting up a sandbox environment, monitoring system calls, and capturing network traffic for analysis. Libraries like subprocess and scapy are useful for automating dynamic analysis tasks.

F. Developing Custom Security Tools

Python's versatility and extensive library ecosystem make it an ideal language for developing custom security tools tailored to specific needs.

- You can create a Python script that evaluates the strength of passwords based on predefined criteria, such as length, complexity, and presence of special characters. This tool can help users generate strong passwords and assess the security of existing ones.
- Python allows you to develop a basic vulnerability scanner that checks for common vulnerabilities in systems or web applications. By leveraging libraries like nmap for network scanning and requests for web requests, you can automate the process of identifying potential security

CHAPTER SEVEN

System Administration

CHAPTER SEVEN OBJECTIVES

After reading this chapter, the reader will be able to:

- Recognize the importance of system administration and asset management in maintaining a secure IT environment.
- Understand the concept of IT assets, their lifecycle stages, and the significance of asset tracking for security, compliance, and cost control.
- Implement various security controls to protect IT assets, including access control, encryption, patch management, and backup and recovery.
- Administer and manage Windows Server and Client operating systems, including remote administration tools.
- Explain the fundamentals of Active Directory (AD) and Active Directory Domain Services (AD DS).
- Configure and manage Group Policy for centralized management and security configuration.
- Apply best practices and considerations when configuring new users and their computers in a simulated career scenario.
- Implement cybersecurity considerations in system administration, such as securing Windows operating systems, Active Directory, and using Group Policy for security configuration management.

ASSET AND INVENTORY MANAGEMENT ESSENTIALS

A. What are IT Assets?

IT assets are any hardware, software, or data components that are owned or used by an organization. Examples include servers, workstations, network devices, software licenses, and databases. Effective asset management is essential for maintaining a secure and efficient IT environment.

B. Why is Asset Tracking Important?

Asset tracking is important for several reasons:

- Knowing what assets you have and where they are located helps you identify potential vulnerabilities and implement appropriate security controls.
- Many industry regulations and standards require organizations to maintain accurate asset inventories and demonstrate effective asset management practices.
- By tracking assets throughout their lifecycle, you can optimize resource allocation, avoid unnecessary purchases, and plan for upgrades and replacements.

ASSET AND INVENTORY MANAGEMENT ESSENTIALS

C. Basic Asset Lifecycle Stages

The asset lifecycle typically consists of the following stages:

- Procurement: Acquiring new assets and adding them to the inventory.
- Deployment: Installing and configuring assets for use in the production environment.
- Maintenance: Monitoring, updating, and repairing assets to ensure optimal performance and security.
- Retirement: Decommissioning and disposing of assets that are no longer needed or have reached the end of their useful life.

D. Securing IT Assets

Securing IT assets involves implementing a combination of physical, technical, and administrative controls, such as:

- Access control: Ensuring that only authorized users can access assets and data.
- Encryption: Protecting sensitive data at rest and in transit using encryption technologies.
- Patch management: Regularly applying security patches and updates to mitigate known vulnerabilities.
- Backup and recovery: Implementing robust backup and disaster recovery processes to ensure data availability and business continuity.

WINDOWS ADMINISTRATION AND MANAGEMENT

A. Introduction to Windows Server and Client operating systems

Windows Server operating systems are designed for running enterprise-level services, such as Active Directory, DNS, and DHCP, while Windows Client operating systems (Windows 10) are optimized for end-user productivity and personal computing.

Windows is widely used in corporate networks due to its extensive features, compatibility with business applications, and centralized management capabilities through Active Directory and Group Policy.

B. Windows Server Administration

To set up a Windows Server, you'll need to choose the appropriate edition, select the installation type (eServer Core or Desktop Experience), and configure basic settings like network adapters, storage, and server roles.

Windows Server uses a role-based installation model, where you can select and configure specific server roles (Active Directory Domain Services, DHCP Server) and features (.NET Framework, Remote Server Administration Tools) based on your organization's requirements.

As a system administrator, you'll be responsible for setting up and maintaining essential network services, such as Dynamic Host Configuration Protocol for IP address allocation and Domain Name System for name resolution.

WINDOWS ADMINISTRATION AND MANAGEMENT

C. Windows Client Administration

You'll need to plan and execute the deployment of Windows client operating systems, such as Windows 10, to end-user devices. This can be done through manual installation, imaging, or automated deployment tools like Microsoft Deployment Toolkit or System Center Configuration Manager.

To ensure proper access control and security, you'll create and manage user accounts, organize them into groups based on roles and responsibilities, and assign appropriate permissions to resources like files, folders, and network shares.

You'll configure security settings on Windows client devices to protect against cyber threats and enforce organizational policies. This includes setting up local security policies, configuring Windows Defender Antivirus, and managing Windows Update settings for timely patching.

WINDOWS ADMINISTRATION AND MANAGEMENT

D. Remote Administration Tools

Windows Remote Desktop Protocol is a built-in protocol that allows you to remotely connect to and manage Windows systems. You can use RDP to access a remote system's desktop, run applications, and perform administrative tasks as if you were sitting in front of the machine.

PowerShell is a powerful scripting language and command-line shell that enables automation and remote management of Windows systems. With PowerShell remoting, you can execute commands and scripts on remote systems, making it an essential tool for efficient system administration.

In addition to built-in tools, there are various third-party remote administration tools available, such as TeamViewer, LogMeIn, and Virtual Network Computing. These tools offer additional features and cross-platform support for remote management of Windows and non-Windows systems.

ACTIVE DIRECTORY AND GROUP POLICY

A. Introduction to Active Directory (AD)

Active Directory is a directory service developed by Microsoft for managing and organizing network resources, such as users, computers, and groups, in a hierarchical structure. AD simplifies administration, enables centralized authentication and authorization, and provides a foundation for other Windows services like Exchange and SharePoint.

AD is organized into logical structures called domains, trees, and forests. A domain is a group of network objects (users, computers) that share a common AD database. Trees are hierarchical structures of domains that share a contiguous namespace, while forests are collections of one or more trees that share a common schema and global catalog.

ACTIVE DIRECTORY AND GROUP POLICY

B. Active Directory Domain Services (AD DS)

To set up Active Directory, you'll need to install the Active Directory Domain Services role on a Windows Server and promote it to a domain controller. During the configuration process, you'll specify the domain name, forest functional level, and other settings based on your organization's requirements.

With AD DS, you can create and manage user accounts and groups in a centralized manner. User accounts represent individual users in the organization, while groups are used to organize users based on roles, departments, or other criteria. You can assign permissions and apply policies to users and groups to control access to resources and enforce security settings.

AD allows you to delegate administrative control over specific domains, organizational units (OU), or resources to other users or groups. This enables you to distribute administrative responsibilities and grant limited access to manage certain aspects of the AD environment without giving full control to everyone.

ACTIVE DIRECTORY AND GROUP POLICY

C. Group Policy Fundamentals

Group Policy is a feature of Active Directory that allows you to centrally manage and enforce configuration settings on computers and users in a domain. GPOs are containers for Group Policy settings that can be linked to domains, OUs, or sites to apply the settings to the objects within them.

To apply Group Policy settings, you'll create GPOs and link them to the appropriate OUs in the AD structure. OUs are containers that can hold users, computers, and other AD objects, allowing you to organize and apply policies based on logical groupings.

GPOs can be used to configure a wide range of security settings and policies, such as password complexity requirements, user rights assignments, security options, and software restriction policies. By leveraging GPOs, you can enforce consistent security configurations across the organization and reduce the risk of misconfigurations or unauthorized changes.

ACTIVE DIRECTORY AND GROUP POLICY

D. Advanced Group Policy Management

Group Policy Preferences is an extension of Group Policy that provides additional settings for managing and configuring Windows systems. With GPP, you can configure registry settings, create shortcuts, map network drives, and perform other tasks that are not available through standard Group Policy settings.

Group Policy Inheritance and Precedence are applied to AD objects based on a hierarchical inheritance model and a specific order of precedence. By default, GPOs linked to higher-level containers are inherited by lower-level containers unless explicitly blocked or overridden. Understanding the inheritance and precedence rules is crucial for effectively managing and troubleshooting Group Policy.

When working with Group Policy, you may encounter various issues, such as settings not being applied, conflicts between GPOs, or slow logon times. To troubleshoot these issues, you can use tools like the Group Policy Management Console, Group Policy Results (gpresult), and Event Viewer to identify and resolve the underlying problems.

CONFIGURING USERS & COMPUTERS

A. Scenario Overview

In this career simulation, you'll be working as a system administrator for a fictional bank called Profyle Credit Union. The company is expanding and has hired several new employees who need to be set up with user accounts and computers. Your task is to configure the new users and their devices in accordance with the company's security policies and best practices.

Your main objectives are to create user accounts in Active Directory, configure appropriate group memberships and permissions, set up GPOs for user and computer settings, and deploy and configure Windows client operating systems on the new devices. You'll need to document your steps and provide a brief report on the completed tasks and any challenges faced during the process.

CONFIGURING USERS & COMPUTERS

B. Step-by-Step Guide

- Begin by creating user accounts for the new employees in Active Directory using the Active Directory Users and Computers console. Ensure that the user names, display names, and email addresses are set up correctly according to the company's naming conventions.
- For each user account, configure the necessary properties, such as password settings, account options, and contact information. Add the users to the appropriate security groups based on their roles and departments to grant them access to the required resources.
- Create new GPOs to enforce the company's security policies and configure user and computer settings. Link the GPOs to the relevant OUs containing the user accounts and computer objects. Configure settings such as password complexity, user rights assignments, and software restriction policies.
- Set up the new computers with the appropriate Windows client operating system (Windows 10) using the company's standard deployment method (imaging or automated deployment). Configure the basic settings, such as network connectivity, system name, and domain membership.
- Use the GPOs created earlier to apply the necessary security policies and settings to the client devices. Verify that the policies are being applied correctly by checking the Group Policy Results on a sample computer.

CONFIGURING USERS & COMPUTERS

C. Best Practices and Considerations

When configuring user accounts and permissions, adhere to the principle of least privilege, granting users only the permissions they need to perform their job functions. This minimizes the potential impact of compromised accounts and helps prevent unauthorized access to sensitive resources.

Ensure that the company's password policies are enforced through GPOs, requiring users to set strong, complex passwords and change them regularly. Consider implementing additional security measures, such as account lockout policies and multi-factor authentication, to further protect user accounts.

Establish a process for periodically reviewing user accounts and permissions to ensure they remain accurate and up-to-date. Remove or disable accounts for employees who have left the company, and adjust permissions as users' roles and responsibilities change over time.

CONFIGURING USERS & COMPUTERS

D. Discussion and Reflection

After completing the career simulation, take some time to reflect on the experience. Consider what you learned about the process of configuring new users and computers, the challenges you encountered, and how you overcame them. Think about how you can apply these lessons to real-world scenarios in your future career as a system administrator.

Discuss the importance of proper user and computer configuration in maintaining a secure and efficient IT environment. Consider how the best practices and techniques covered in the simulation can be applied to various organizations and industries, and how they contribute to overall cybersecurity efforts.

SYSTEM ADMINISTRATION

A. Securing Windows Server and Client operating systems

Regularly apply security updates and patches to Windows Server and Client operating systems to address known vulnerabilities and protect against emerging threats. Establish a patch management process to ensure that all systems are kept up-to-date and secure.

Implement security best practices and guidelines to harden the configuration of Windows Server and Client operating systems. This includes disabling unnecessary services, configuring secure default settings, and using security templates or baselines to consistently apply security configurations across the environment.

Use access controls and permissions to restrict access to sensitive resources and limit the potential impact of compromised accounts. Implement the principle of least privilege, granting users only the permissions they need to perform their job functions, and regularly review and update permissions as needed.

SYSTEM ADMINISTRATION

B. Securing Active Directory

Prioritize the security of privileged accounts, such as domain administrators and enterprise administrators, as they have extensive control over the AD environment. Implement strong password policies, enable multi-factor authentication, and limit the number of privileged accounts to reduce the risk of compromise.

Enable auditing and monitoring of Active Directory activities to detect and investigate suspicious or malicious actions. Use tools like Event Viewer, security information and event management solutions, and AD-specific monitoring tools to track changes, access attempts, and other relevant events.

Strengthen the security of Active Directory by implementing multi-factor authentication for user accounts, especially privileged accounts. MFA adds an extra layer of protection by requiring users to provide additional verification factors, such as a one-time code or biometric data, in addition to their password.

SYSTEM ADMINISTRATION

C. Using Group Policy for Security Configuration Management

Leverage Group Policy to enforce and maintain consistent security policies across the organization. Use GPOs to configure security settings, such as password policies, user rights assignments, and security options, ensuring that all systems adhere to the company's security standards.

Implement application whitelisting or blacklisting through Group Policy to control which applications can run on client devices. Whitelisting allows only approved applications to execute, while blacklisting blocks known malicious or unauthorized applications. This helps prevent the execution of malware and reduces the risk of security incidents.

Use security baselines and compliance policies to establish a minimum level of security configuration for systems in the organization. Microsoft provides security baselines for Windows Server and Client operating systems, which can be customized to meet specific organizational requirements. Regularly assess and update these baselines to ensure they align with the latest security best practices and regulatory standards.

CHAPTER EIGHT

Defense Security Controls

CHAPTER EIGHT OBJECTIVES

After reading this chapter, the reader will be able to:

- Understand the concept of defense in depth and its role in mitigating cyber risks
- Identify and differentiate between various network security controls, such as firewalls, intrusion prevention systems (IPS), and virtual private networks (VPNs)
- Implement host and endpoint protection measures, including anti-malware solutions, host-based firewalls, and application whitelisting
- Apply access controls and identity management best practices, such as multi-factor authentication (MFA), role-based access control (RBAC), and biometric authentication
- Understand the fundamentals of encryption and key management, including symmetric and asymmetric encryption, public key infrastructure (PKI), and key management best practices
- Develop and maintain effective patch management and system hardening processes to reduce vulnerabilities and enhance overall security posture

NETWORKING SECURITY CONTROLS

A. Firewalls

1. Types of firewalls:

- Stateful firewalls monitor and track the state of network connections, allowing or blocking traffic based on predefined rules and the context of the connection.
- Next-generation firewalls combine traditional firewall capabilities with advanced features, such as deep packet inspection , intrusion prevention, and application awareness.
- Application-layer firewalls operate at the application layer of the OSI model, providing granular control over specific applications and protocols.

2. Firewall placement and architecture:

- Perimeter firewalls are placed at the network boundary to control traffic between the internal network and the internet.
- Internal firewalls are used to segment the network and control traffic between different security zones or departments.
- Demilitarized zones are isolated network segments that host externally-facing services, such as web servers, while providing an additional layer of security.

3. Firewall rules and configuration best practices:

- Implement a default-deny policy, where all traffic is blocked unless explicitly allowed.
- Use the principle of least privilege when defining firewall rules, granting access only to necessary services and ports.
- Regularly review and update firewall rules to ensure they align with the organization's security policies and business requirements.

NETWORKING SECURITY CONTROLS

B. Intrusion Prevention Systems and Intrusion Detection Systems

1. The difference between IPS and IDS:

- Intrusion Detection Systems monitor network traffic for suspicious activities and generate alerts when potential threats are detected, but do not actively block the traffic.
- Intrusion Prevention Systems build upon IDS capabilities by actively blocking or dropping malicious traffic in real-time, based on predefined rules and signatures.

2. Signature-based vs. anomaly-based detection:

- Signature-based detection relies on a database of known attack patterns and malware signatures to identify threats.
- Anomaly-based detection uses machine learning and statistical analysis to identify deviations from normal network behavior, enabling the detection of previously unknown or "zero-day" threats.

3. Placement and integration with other security controls:

- Network-based IPS/IDS are typically placed at strategic points within the network, such as the perimeter or between security zones.
- Host-based IPS/IDS are installed on individual servers or endpoints to monitor and protect specific systems.
- Integration with other security controls, such as firewalls and security information and event management systems, enables a more comprehensive and coordinated defense.

NETWORKING SECURITY CONTROLS

C. Virtual Private Networks

1. Remote access VPNs:

- Remote access VPNs allow individual users to securely connect to an organization's network from remote locations, such as home or public Wi-Fi hotspots.
- They encrypt the user's internet traffic and create a secure tunnel between the user's device and the organization's network, protecting sensitive data from interception and eavesdropping.

2. Site-to-site VPNs:

- Site-to-site VPNs establish a secure connection between two or more networks, such as branch offices or remote data centers.
- They enable the secure exchange of data and resources between sites, creating a virtual extension of the organization's network.

3. VPN protocols and encryption:

- Common VPN protocols include IPsec, SSL/TLS, and PPTP, each with different security features and performance characteristics.
- VPNs use encryption algorithms, such as AES or Blowfish, to protect data in transit and ensure confidentiality and integrity.

HOST AND ENDPOINT PROTECTION

A. Anti-Malware Solutions

1. Signature-based vs. behavior-based detection:

- Signature-based anti-malware solutions rely on a database of known malware signatures to identify and block threats.
- Behavior-based detection analyzes the actions and patterns of programs to identify suspicious or malicious behavior, enabling the detection of previously unknown or polymorphic malware.

2. Endpoint Detection and Response (EDR) capabilities:

- EDR solutions provide advanced threat detection, investigation, and response capabilities for endpoints, such as laptops, desktops, and servers.
- They collect and analyze endpoint data, including system events, network activity, and file changes, to identify and respond to potential threats in real-time.

3. Integration with centralized management and reporting:

- Centralized management consoles allow administrators to deploy, configure, and update anti-malware solutions across the organization from a single interface.
- Integration with SIEM systems and other security tools enables consolidated reporting, incident response, and threat hunting capabilities.

HOST AND ENDPOINT PROTECTION

B. Host-based Firewalls

1. Benefits and limitations of host-based firewalls:

- Host-based firewalls provide an additional layer of defense at the individual system level, complementing network-based firewalls.
- They can control inbound and outbound traffic for specific applications and services, reducing the attack surface of the host.
- However, host-based firewalls may be more challenging to manage and maintain consistently across a large number of systems.

2. Configuration and policy management:

- Centralized management tools and group policies can help ensure consistent configuration and enforcement of host-based firewall rules across the organization.
- Regular reviews and updates of host-based firewall policies are necessary to maintain their effectiveness and alignment with the organization's security requirements.

HOST AND ENDPOINT PROTECTION

C. Application Whitelisting

1. Allow-listing vs. block-listing approaches:

- Application whitelisting (allow-listing) is a security approach that permits only explicitly approved applications to run on a system, blocking all others by default.
- Block-listing, on the other hand, attempts to prevent known malicious applications from running, while allowing all other applications by default.

2. Application control and zero-trust execution:

- Application control solutions enforce whitelisting policies and provide granular control over which applications and processes are allowed to run on a system.
- Zero-trust execution takes this concept further by treating all applications and processes as untrusted and requiring them to be explicitly authorized and validated before execution.

ACCESS CONTROLS AND IDENTITY MANAGEMENT

A. Multi-Factor Authentication

1. The three factors of authentication:

- Something you know (password, PIN)
- Something you have (token, smart card)
- Something you are (fingerprint, facial recognition)

2. Common MFA methods:

- Hardware tokens generate one-time passwords that users must provide in addition to their regular credentials.
- Smart cards contain digital certificates that authenticate users and can be used in conjunction with PINs or biometric factors.
- Biometric factors, such as fingerprints or facial recognition, provide a unique and convenient way to authenticate users based on their physical characteristics.

3. Implementing MFA for remote access and privileged accounts:

- MFA should be mandatory for remote access to an organization's network and resources, as well as for privileged accounts with elevated permissions.
- Implementing MFA for these high-risk scenarios adds an extra layer of security and helps prevent unauthorized access, even if a user's password is compromised.

ACCESS CONTROLS AND IDENTITY MANAGEMENT

B. Role-Based Access Control

1. The principle of least privilege:

- The principle of least privilege states that users should be granted the minimum level of access necessary to perform their job functions.
- This approach minimizes the potential impact of a compromised account and helps prevent unauthorized access to sensitive resources.

2. Defining roles and permissions:

- RBAC involves defining roles based on job functions and assigning permissions to those roles, rather than individual users.
- Roles should be carefully designed to ensure that users have access to the resources they need, while still adhering to the principle of least privilege.

3. Implementing RBAC in directory services and applications:

- Directory services, such as Active Directory or LDAP, can be used to define and manage roles and permissions across an organization.
- Applications and systems should be configured to integrate with directory services and enforce RBAC policies consistently.

ACCESS CONTROLS AND IDENTITY MANAGEMENT

C. Biometric Authentication

1. Types of biometric factors:

- Fingerprint recognition uses the unique patterns of a user's fingerprints to authenticate their identity.
- Facial recognition analyzes the unique characteristics of a user's face, such as the distance between their eyes and the shape of their jaw, to verify their identity.
- Other biometric factors include iris recognition, voice recognition, and behavioral biometrics (typing patterns).

2. Benefits and challenges of biometric authentication:

- Biometric authentication provides a convenient and secure way to verify a user's identity, as biometric factors are unique and difficult to forge or steal.
- However, biometric data is sensitive and must be carefully protected to prevent unauthorized access or misuse.
- Biometric systems may also face challenges related to accuracy, performance, and user acceptance.

ACCESS CONTROLS AND IDENTITY MANAGEMENT

D. Identity and Access Management Best Practices

1. Centralizing IAM across the organization:

- Centralizing IAM helps ensure consistent policies and control over user identities and access rights across an organization's systems and applications.
- Centralized IAM solutions, such as single sign-on and federated identity management, can streamline user authentication and access management processes.

2. Implementing single sign-on:

- SSO allows users to authenticate once and access multiple applications and resources without having to re-enter their credentials.
- SSO improves user experience and productivity while reducing the risk of password fatigue and weak password practices.

3. Conducting regular access reviews and audits:

- Regular access reviews and audits help ensure that user access rights remain appropriate and aligned with their job functions and organizational policies.
- Access reviews should be conducted periodically (quarterly or annually) and whenever a user's role or employment status changes.

ENCRYPTION AND KEY MANAGEMENT

A. Overview of Encryption Algorithms and Protocols

1. Symmetric vs. asymmetric encryption:

- Symmetric encryption uses a single key for both encrypting and decrypting data. Examples include AES and 3DES.
- Asymmetric encryption, also known as public-key cryptography, uses a pair of keys (public and private) for encryption and decryption. Examples include RSA and ECC.

2. Block ciphers and stream ciphers:

- Block ciphers encrypt data in fixed-size blocks, typically 64 or 128 bits. Examples include AES and Blowfish.
- Stream ciphers encrypt data one bit or byte at a time, generating a pseudorandom stream of bits that is combined with the plaintext. Examples include RC4 and ChaCha20.

3. Key exchange protocols:

- Key exchange protocols, such as Diffie-Hellman, enable two parties to securely establish a shared secret key over an insecure channel, without the need for prior key distribution.

ENCRYPTION AND KEY MANAGEMENT

B. Public Key Infrastructure

1. The role of certificates and certificate authorities:

- Digital certificates are electronic documents that bind a public key to an identity, providing a means to verify the authenticity of the key and its owner.
- Certificate authorities are trusted third parties that issue, manage, and revoke digital certificates, establishing trust in the public key infrastructure.

2. PKI hierarchies and trust models:

- PKI hierarchies define the relationships between CAs and the certificates they issue, creating a chain of trust from root CAs to end-entity certificates.
- Trust models, such as the web of trust and the hierarchical trust model, determine how certificates are validated and trusted within a PKI ecosystem.

3. Implementing PKI for email, web, and document signing:

- PKI can be used to secure email communication through the use of S/MIME certificates, encrypting and signing email messages to ensure confidentiality, integrity, and non-repudiation.
- SSL/TLS certificates are used to secure web traffic, providing encryption and authentication for websites and web applications.
- Digital signatures, based on PKI, can be used to ensure the integrity and authenticity of electronic documents and software packages.

ENCRYPTION AND KEY MANAGEMENT

C. Key Management

1. Key generation, distribution, and storage:

- Secure key generation involves using cryptographically secure random number generators and adhering to best practices for key length and algorithm selection.
- Key distribution must be performed over secure channels, such as encrypted network connections or physical key exchange ceremonies, to prevent interception or tampering.
- Key storage should employ hardware security modules or secure key management systems to protect keys from unauthorized access or theft.

2. Hardware security modules and key management systems:

- HSMs are physical devices that provide secure key generation, storage, and cryptographic operations, protecting keys from software-based attacks and insider threats.
- Key management systems centralize the lifecycle management of cryptographic keys, including generation, distribution, rotation, and retirement, ensuring consistent and secure key handling across an organization.

3. Lifecycle management and key rotation:

- Key lifecycle management involves defining and enforcing policies for key creation, usage, expiration, and destruction, based on the organization's security requirements and industry best practices.
- Key rotation is the process of periodically replacing cryptographic keys to limit the potential impact of key compromise and ensure forward secrecy.

PATCH MANAGEMENT AND SYSTEM HACKING

A. The Importance of Patch Management

1. Vulnerability management and patch prioritization:

- Vulnerability management involves identifying, assessing, and prioritizing vulnerabilities in an organization's systems and applications.
- Patch prioritization helps organizations determine which patches to apply first, based on factors such as the criticality of the vulnerability, the likelihood of exploitation, and the potential impact on the business.

2. Automated vs. manual patching processes:

- Automated patch management tools can streamline the process of identifying, downloading, and installing patches across an organization's systems, reducing the time and effort required for manual patching.
- However, some patches may require manual intervention, such as those that impact critical systems or require specific testing and validation procedures.

3. Testing and validation of patches:

- Patch testing and validation are essential to ensure that patches do not introduce new issues or incompatibilities with existing systems and applications.
- Organizations should establish a testing environment that mirrors their production systems to thoroughly test patches before deployment.

PATCH MANAGEMENT AND SYSTEM HACKING

B. System Hardening Techniques

1. Reducing attack surface and disabling unnecessary services:

- Reducing the attack surface involves identifying and eliminating unnecessary services, applications, and network ports that could be exploited by attackers.
- Disabling or uninstalling unused services and applications helps minimize the potential entry points for attackers and reduces the risk of vulnerabilities.

2. Hardening operating systems and applications:

- OS hardening involves configuring security settings, disabling default accounts, and applying security templates or baselines to ensure

CHAPTER NINE

Red Team Offense

CHAPTER NINE OBJECTIVES

After reading this chapter, the reader will be able to:

- Understand the importance of offensive security in strengthening an organization's defenses
- Identify and exploit common web application vulnerabilities, such as injection flaws and cross-site scripting
- Apply a structured penetration testing methodology to assess the security of systems and applications
- Recognize and employ various social engineering techniques to test an organization's human defenses
- Use popular web application penetration testing tools, such as Burp Suite and OWASP ZAP, to identify and exploit vulnerabilities
- Leverage the Metasploit Framework for vulnerability exploitation and post-exploitation activities
- Conduct a mock penetration test, simulating a real-world engagement from planning to reporting

WEB APPLICATION VULNERABILITIES

1. Injection flaws:

Injection flaws occur when untrusted user input is sent to an interpreter as part of a command or query. Attackers can exploit these flaws to execute arbitrary commands or access sensitive data. For example, an SQL injection vulnerability in a login form could allow an attacker to bypass authentication and gain unauthorized access to the application.

2. Cross-Site Scripting (XSS):

XSS vulnerabilities allow attackers to inject malicious scripts into web pages viewed by other users. These scripts can steal sensitive information, such as session tokens or passwords, or perform actions on behalf of the victim. There are three main types of XSS: reflected, stored, and DOM-based.

WEB APPLICATION VULNERABILITIES

4. Broken Authentication and Session Management:

Weaknesses in an application's authentication and session management mechanisms can allow attackers to compromise user accounts, steal session tokens, or gain unauthorized access. Examples include weak password policies, unprotected session tokens, and lack of proper session expiration.

5. Sensitive Data Exposure:

Applications that fail to properly protect sensitive data, such as financial information or personal details, can expose users to identity theft, fraud, or other harms. Common causes include unencrypted data transmission, weak encryption algorithms, or improper handling of encryption keys.

6. Insufficient Logging and Monitoring:

Inadequate logging and monitoring can prevent an organization from detecting and responding to security incidents in a timely manner. Attackers can exploit this lack of visibility to carry out malicious activities undetected, potentially leading to significant damage or data loss.

WEB APPLICATION VULNERABILITIES

C. OWASP Top 10

1. Overview of the OWASP Top 10 project:

The Open Web Application Security Project Top 10 is a widely recognized awareness document that highlights the most critical security risks facing web applications. Updated regularly, the OWASP Top 10 provides a prioritized list of the most common and impactful web application vulnerabilities, along with recommendations for mitigating these risks.

2. Detailed analysis of each vulnerability category:

The OWASP Top 10 provides a detailed description of each vulnerability category, including its prevalence, technical impacts, and common attack scenarios. By understanding these vulnerabilities in-depth, offensive security professionals can more effectively identify and exploit them during testing engagements.

3. Real-world examples and case studies:

To illustrate the potential impact of OWASP Top 10 vulnerabilities, the document includes real-world examples and case studies. These examples help readers understand how attackers can exploit these vulnerabilities and the consequences for affected organizations.

Example case study: In 2017, the credit reporting agency Equifax suffered a massive data breach due to an unpatched vulnerability in the Apache Struts web framework. The breach exposed the personal information of over 147 million people, highlighting the importance of timely patching and vulnerability management.

PENETRATION TESTING METHODOLOGY

A. Overview of penetration testing

1. Objectives and scope of penetration testing:

Penetration testing is a simulated attack on a system, network, or application to evaluate its security posture. The primary objectives of penetration testing are to identify vulnerabilities, assess the potential impact of a breach, and provide recommendations for remediation. The scope of a penetration test can vary depending on the organization's requirements and may include internal systems, external-facing applications, or wireless networks.

2. Types of penetration testing:

- Black-box testing: Testers have no prior knowledge of the target system and must rely on publicly available information and their own skills to identify vulnerabilities. This type of testing simulates an external attacker's perspective.
- White-box testing: Testers are provided with full access to the target system's source code, architecture, and documentation. This type of testing is more comprehensive and can identify deeper vulnerabilities.
- Gray-box testing: Testers have partial knowledge of the target system, often equivalent to that of an authenticated user. This type of testing can simulate insider threats or attacks by users with limited privileges.

PENETRATION TESTING METHODOLOGY

B. Penetration testing phases

1. Planning and Reconnaissance:

In this phase, testers gather information about the target system, such as IP addresses, domain names, and publicly available data. They also work with the organization to define the scope, objectives, and rules of engagement for the testing process.

2. Scanning and Enumeration:

Testers use automated tools and manual techniques to scan the target system for open ports, running services, and potential vulnerabilities. They also enumerate the system to identify user accounts, network shares, and other valuable information.

3. Vulnerability Assessment:

Based on the results of the scanning and enumeration phase, testers analyze the identified vulnerabilities to determine their severity and potential impact. They prioritize the vulnerabilities based on factors such as ease of exploitation and potential damage.

PENETRATION TESTING METHODOLOGY

4. Exploitation and Post-Exploitation:

In this phase, testers attempt to exploit the identified vulnerabilities to gain unauthorized access or escalate privileges. Once they have gained access, they perform post-exploitation activities, such as data exfiltration or lateral movement, to assess the potential impact of a successful breach.

5. Reporting and Remediation:

Finally, testers prepare a comprehensive report detailing their findings, including the identified vulnerabilities, the methods used to exploit them, and recommendations for remediation. They may also provide guidance on prioritizing remediation efforts based on the risk level of each vulnerability.

PENETRATION TESTING METHODOLOGY

C. Penetration testing standards and frameworks

1. NIST SP 800-115:

The National Institute of Standards and Technology Special Publication 800-115, "Technical Guide to Information Security Testing and Assessment," provides guidelines for planning and conducting information security tests and assessments, including penetration testing. It outlines a four-phase approach: planning, discovery, attack, and reporting.

2. OWASP Testing Guide:

The OWASP Testing Guide is a comprehensive manual for web application security testing. It covers various testing techniques, tools, and best practices, and is organized around the OWASP Top 10 vulnerabilities. The guide serves as a valuable resource for penetration testers and developers looking to ensure the security of their web applications.

3. Penetration Testing Execution Standard:

PTES is a comprehensive framework that outlines seven main sections of a penetration test: pre-engagement interactions, intelligence gathering, threat modeling, vulnerability analysis, exploitation, post-exploitation, and reporting. It provides a standardized approach to conducting penetration tests and ensuring consistency across different testers and engagements.

SOCIAL ENGINEERING TECHNIQUES

A. Overview of social engineering

1. Psychological principles behind social engineering:

Social engineering relies on manipulating human psychology to trick individuals into divulging sensitive information or performing actions that compromise security.

Some common psychological principles exploited by social engineers include:

- Authority: People tend to comply with requests from those in positions of authority.
- Scarcity: The perceived scarcity of an item or opportunity can lead people to make hasty decisions.
- Social proof: People are more likely to engage in behaviors that they believe others are engaging in.
- Liking: People are more likely to comply with requests from individuals they like or perceive as similar to themselves.

2. Types of social engineering attacks:

- Phishing: Sending fraudulent emails or messages that appear to be from a trustworthy source to trick recipients into revealing sensitive information or clicking on malicious links.
- Pretexting: Creating a fabricated scenario to deceive a target into providing sensitive information or access.
- Baiting: Offering something enticing, such as a free gift or download, to lure targets into compromising their security.
- Tailgating: Gaining unauthorized access to a secure area by following closely behind an authorized individual.

SOCIAL ENGINEERING TECHNIQUES

B. Phishing and Spear-Phishing

1. Email-based phishing:

Email phishing attacks involve sending mass emails that appear to be from legitimate organizations, such as banks or service providers, to trick recipients into revealing sensitive information or clicking on malicious links. These emails often use urgent language, threatening consequences for non-compliance, or promising rewards to increase the likelihood of the target falling for the scam.

Example phishing email:

Dear [Victim],

We have detected suspicious activity on your account. To avoid permanent suspension, please click the link below and verify your account information:

[Malicious Link]

If you do not verify your account within 24 hours, your access will be permanently revoked.

Thank you for your cooperation,
[Spoofed Company Name]

SOCIAL ENGINEERING TECHNIQUES

2. SMS phishing:

SMS phishing involves sending fraudulent text messages to trick recipients into revealing sensitive information or installing malicious software on their mobile devices. These messages often use similar tactics to email phishing, such as creating a sense of urgency or impersonating trusted entities.

Example SMiShing message:

Your package has been delayed. Please click the link to update your delivery information and avoid additional fees: [Malicious Link]

3. Voice phishing:

Voice phishing, or vishing, involves using phone calls to deceive targets into revealing sensitive information or performing actions that compromise security. Attackers may impersonate technical support representatives, bank employees, or government officials to lend credibility to their requests.

Example vishing script:

Hello, this is [Spoofed Name] from the [Spoofed Company] fraud department. We have detected suspicious activity on your account. To verify your identity and secure your account, please provide me with your full name, date of birth, and social security number.

PHYSICAL SOCIAL ENGINEERING

C. Physical Social Engineering

1. Tailgating and piggybacking:

Tailgating and piggybacking involve gaining unauthorized access to a secure area by following closely behind an authorized individual. Attackers may impersonate delivery personnel, maintenance workers, or other trusted roles to avoid suspicion.

Example scenario: An attacker, dressed as a delivery person with a large package, waits outside a secure office building. When an employee opens the door to leave, the attacker quickly follows behind, claiming to be making a delivery to a specific office.

2. Dumpster diving:

Dumpster diving involves searching through an organization's trash or recycling bins to find sensitive information, such as discarded documents, notes, or old hardware. Attackers can use this information to gain insight into the organization's systems, employees, or security practices.

Example scenario: An attacker searches through a company's dumpster and finds a discarded employee directory, which includes names, job titles, and contact information. The attacker uses this information to craft targeted phishing emails or to impersonate employees during social engineering attacks.

PHYSICAL SOCIAL ENGINEERING

3. Impersonation and pretexting:

Impersonation and pretexting involve creating a fabricated scenario or identity to deceive a target into providing sensitive information or access. Attackers may pose as IT support personnel, auditors, or other trusted roles to lend credibility to their requests.

Example scenario: An attacker calls an organization's help desk, claiming to be a new employee who needs assistance setting up their account. The attacker provides a convincing pretext, such as being in a rush to prepare for an important meeting, and convinces the help desk representative to reset their password over the phone.

PHYSICAL SOCIAL ENGINEERING

D. Countermeasures and awareness training

To defend against social engineering attacks, organizations should implement a combination of technical controls and employee awareness training.

Some key countermeasures include:

- Implementing strong authentication methods, such as multi-factor authentication, to prevent unauthorized access even if credentials are compromised.
- Establishing clear policies and procedures for handling sensitive information and responding to suspicious requests.
- Conducting regular employee awareness training to educate staff on recognizing and reporting social engineering attempts.
- Implementing email filters and anti-phishing tools to reduce the likelihood of successful phishing attacks.
- Encouraging a culture of security awareness and vigilance, where employees feel empowered to question suspicious activities and report potential incidents without fear of retribution.

PENETRATION TESTING TOOLS

A. Burp Suite

1. Introduction to Burp Suite:

Burp Suite is a popular web application penetration testing platform that provides a comprehensive set of tools for analyzing and exploiting web applications. It is widely used by security professionals and researchers to identify vulnerabilities, manipulate requests and responses, and automate testing processes.

2. Setting up and configuring Burp Suite:

To use Burp Suite effectively, testers must configure their browser to proxy traffic through Burp and set up the appropriate SSL certificates. They can then use Burp's various tools, such as the Proxy, Spider, and Scanner, to intercept and modify web traffic, map the application's structure, and identify potential vulnerabilities.

3. Using Burp Suite for web application testing:

Burp Suite's tools can be used to perform a wide range of testing activities, such as:
- Intercepting and modifying HTTP requests and responses to test for input validation flaws or injection vulnerabilities.
- Using the Spider tool to automatically map the application's structure and discover hidden pages or functionality.
- Employing the Scanner to automatically identify common vulnerabilities, such as SQL injection or cross-site scripting.
- Leveraging the Repeater tool to manually modify and resend individual requests for more targeted testing.

PENETRATION TESTING TOOLS

B. Cross-Site Scripting Exploitation

1. Types of XSS:

- Reflected XSS: Occurs when user input is immediately returned by the web application and executed in the victim's browser.
- Stored XSS: Happens when user input is stored by the application (in a database) and later retrieved and executed in the victim's browser

CHAPTER TEN

Blue Team Offense

CHAPTER TEN OBJECTIVES

After reading this chapter, the reader will be able to:

- Understand the importance of logging and log analysis in detecting and investigating security incidents
- Apply log analysis techniques to identify anomalies and correlate events across multiple log sources
- Utilize Security Information and Event Management (SIEM) solutions for centralized log management and threat detection
- Understand the fundamentals of digital forensics and incident response, including the digital forensics process and incident response lifecycle
- Employ digital forensics and incident response tools and techniques to investigate and resolve security incidents
- Comprehend the NIST Cybersecurity Framework and its role in assessing and improving an organization's cybersecurity posture
- Apply the knowledge and skills gained from the chapter to real-world scenarios, such as solving a configuration file problem as a SOC analyst

LOGGING AND LOG ANALYSIS

A. The importance of logging in detecting and investigating security incidents

Logging is the process of recording events and activities that occur within an organization's systems, networks, and applications. It plays a crucial role in detecting and investigating security incidents by providing valuable information about:

1. Types of logs:

- System logs: Record events related to the operating system, such as user logins, system errors, and service start/stop events.
- Application logs: Capture events specific to individual applications, such as user actions, errors, and performance metrics.
- Security logs: Record security-related events, such as failed login attempts, access control changes, and malware detections.

2. Log management best practices:

- Centralized log collection: Aggregating logs from multiple sources into a central repository for easier analysis and correlation.
- Log retention: Storing logs for an appropriate period to ensure they are available for incident investigation and compliance purposes.
- Log protection: Securing logs from unauthorized access, modification, or deletion to maintain their integrity and confidentiality.

Example log entry:

2023-04-15 14:32:15 Host: 192.168.1.100 User: john.doe Event: Login_Success

LOGGING AND LOG ANALYSIS

B. Log analysis techniques

Log analysis involves examining log data to identify patterns, anomalies, and indicators of compromise (IoC).

Some common techniques include:

1. Identifying baseline behavior and anomalies:

- Establishing a baseline of normal system and user behavior to detect deviations that may indicate a security incident.
- Using statistical analysis and machine learning algorithms to identify anomalies in log data.

2. Correlating events across multiple log sources:

- Combining log data from different sources (system logs, application logs, and security logs) to gain a more comprehensive view of an incident.
- Using correlation rules and algorithms to identify related events and build a timeline of an incident.

3. Using regular expressions and filters to search for specific patterns:

- Employing regular expressions to search for specific patterns in log data, such as IP addresses, domain names, or error codes.
- Applying filters to narrow down log data based on criteria like time range, event type, or source.

LOGGING AND LOG ANALYSIS

C. Security Information and Event Management solutions

SIEM solutions are designed to collect, analyze, and correlate log data from various sources to detect and respond to security incidents.

1. Introduction to SIEM concepts and architecture:

SIEM solutions typically consist of log collection agents, a central log repository, an analysis engine, and a user interface for visualization and reporting. They use a combination of rule-based and anomaly-based detection methods to identify potential security incidents.

2. Popular SIEM solutions:

- Splunk: A widely-used platform for log management, analysis, and visualization, with a strong focus on security use cases.
- ELK Stack: An open-source solution combining Elasticsearch, Logstash, and Kibana for log collection, analysis, and visualization.
- IBM QRadar: An enterprise SIEM solution that provides advanced threat detection, incident forensics, and compliance reporting capabilities.

LOGGING AND LOG ANALYSIS

3. Configuring and using Splunk for log analysis and threat detection:

- Installing and configuring Splunk components, such as forwarders and indexers, to collect and centralize log data.
- Creating Splunk searches and dashboards to analyze log data and visualize security events.
- Configuring Splunk alerts and correlation searches to detect and respond to potential security incidents.

Example Splunk search to find failed login attempts:

sourcetype="windows_security" EventCode=4625

DIGITAL FORENSICS AND INCIDENT RESPONSE

A. Introduction to digital forensics

Digital forensics is the practice of collecting, analyzing, and preserving digital evidence to investigate cyber incidents and support legal proceedings.

1. The role of digital forensics in cybersecurity:

- Identifying the cause, scope, and impact of a security incident
- Gathering evidence to support incident response and remediation efforts
- Providing digital evidence for legal and regulatory compliance purposes

2. The digital forensics process:

- Collection: Identifying and acquiring digital evidence in a forensically sound manner
- Examination: Processing and analyzing the collected evidence to identify relevant information
- Analysis: Drawing conclusions and insights from the examined evidence
- Reporting: Documenting the findings and presenting them to stakeholders

3. Legal considerations and chain of custody:

- Ensuring the admissibility of digital evidence in court by following proper legal procedures and maintaining a clear chain of custody
- Obtaining necessary legal authorizations, such as search warrants or subpoenas, to collect and examine digital evidence

DIGITAL FORENSICS AND INCIDENT RESPONSE

B. Incident response fundamentals

Incident response is the process of detecting, investigating, and mitigating cyber incidents to minimize their impact on an organization.

1. Incident response planning and preparation:

- Developing an incident response plan that outlines roles, responsibilities, and procedures for handling incidents
- Forming an incident response team with the necessary skills and expertise
- Conducting incident response training and tabletop exercises to test and refine the plan

2. Incident detection and analysis:

- Monitoring systems and logs for indicators of compromise and anomalous activity
- Triaging and prioritizing incidents based on their potential impact and severity
- Analyzing incidents to determine their scope, cause, and effects

DIGITAL FORENSICS AND INCIDENT RESPONSE

3. Containment, eradication, and recovery:

- Isolating affected systems to prevent further damage and limit the spread of the incident
- Removing malware, closing vulnerabilities, and restoring systems to a secure state
- Recovering data from backups and resuming normal business operations

4. Post-incident activity and lessons learned:

- Conducting a post-incident review to identify strengths, weaknesses, and areas for improvement in the incident response process
- Updating the incident response plan and security controls based on the lessons learned
- Communicating the incident and response efforts to stakeholders and management.

DIGITAL FORENSICS AND INCIDENT RESPONSE

C. Digital forensics and incident response tools and techniques

1. Disk imaging and memory acquisition:

- Using tools like FTK Imager or dd to create forensically sound copies of hard drives and memory for analysis
- Ensuring the integrity of the acquired evidence through hashing and write-blocking techniques

2. Network traffic analysis and packet capturing:

- Utilizing tools like Wireshark or tcpdump to capture and analyze network traffic for signs of malicious activity
- Identifying suspicious connections, protocols, and payloads that may indicate a security incident

3. Malware analysis and reverse engineering:

- Examining malware samples to understand their behavior, functionality, and indicators of compromise
- Using static and dynamic analysis techniques, such as disassembly and debugging, to reverse engineer malware code

Example memory acquisition command using dd:

```
dd if=/dev/mem of=memory.img bs=1MB
```

NIST CYBERSECURITY FRAMEWORK

A. Introduction to the NIST Cybersecurity Framework

The NIST Cybersecurity Framework is a voluntary guidance framework developed by the National Institute of Standards and Technology to help organizations manage and reduce cybersecurity risk.

1. History and purpose of the framework:

- Developed in response to Executive Order 13636, "Improving Critical Infrastructure Cybersecurity," in 2014
- Provides a common language and methodology for understanding, managing, and expressing cybersecurity risk

2. The five core functions:

- Identify: Understanding the organization's assets, systems, and risks
- Protect: Implementing appropriate safeguards to ensure the delivery of critical services
- Detect: Identifying the occurrence of a cybersecurity event in a timely manner
- Respond: Taking action regarding a detected cybersecurity incident
- Recover: Maintaining plans for resilience and restoring capabilities or services impaired due to a cybersecurity incident

NIST CYBERSECURITY FRAMEWORK

B. Implementing the NIST Cybersecurity Framework

1. Mapping the framework to an organization's existing security practices:

- Aligning the organization's current cybersecurity practices with the framework's categories and subcategories
- Identifying gaps and areas for improvement in the organization's cybersecurity posture

2. Using the framework to assess and improve cybersecurity posture:

- Conducting a self-assessment using the framework's tiers to determine the organization's current cybersecurity maturity level
- Developing a target profile that represents the desired state of cybersecurity for the organization
- Creating an action plan to close the gaps between the current and target profiles

3. Communicating cybersecurity risk and maturity to stakeholders:

- Using the framework's common language to communicate cybersecurity risk and maturity to executive management, board members, and other stakeholders
- Demonstrating the organization's commitment to cybersecurity and compliance with industry standards and regulations

NIST CYBERSECURITY FRAMEWORK

C. Case studies and real-world examples of NIST Cybersecurity Framework adoption

Example 1: A large financial institution adopts the NIST Cybersecurity

Framework to align its cybersecurity practices with industry standards and regulatory requirements. By conducting a self-assessment and developing a target profile, the institution identifies areas for improvement and creates an action plan to enhance its cybersecurity posture.

Example 2: A healthcare provider uses the NIST Cybersecurity

Framework to assess its cybersecurity maturity and communicate risk to its board of directors. By demonstrating its alignment with the framework, the provider builds trust with its patients and partners, and ensures compliance with HIPAA regulations.

SOLVING CONFIGURATION FILE ISSUES

A. Scenario background and problem statement

1. Organization and team structure:

- Profyle Tech Inc., a mid-sized technology company with a dedicated Security Operations Center team
- The SOC team consists of analysts, engineers, and a manager, responsible for monitoring and protecting the company's assets and infrastructure

2. Description of the configuration file issue and its impact:

- A critical application server has been experiencing intermittent outages and performance issues
- The server's configuration file has been identified as a potential cause of the problem
- The outages have disrupted business operations and caused frustration among users

SOLVING CONFIGURATION FILE ISSUES

B. Step-by-step walkthrough

1. Identifying and prioritizing the incident:

- SOC analyst receives an alert about the application server's outages and performance issues
- Analyst assesses the impact and severity of the incident and prioritizes it for investigation

2. Gathering and analyzing relevant logs and data sources:

- Analyst collects logs from the application server, operating system, and network devices
- Using a SIEM solution, the analyst correlates events across multiple log sources to identify patterns and anomalies

3. Determining the root cause and scope of the issue:

- Analyst identifies suspicious entries in the application server's configuration file
- Further analysis reveals that the configuration file has been modified by an unauthorized user, causing the performance issues

SOLVING CONFIGURATION FILE ISSUES

4. Implementing and testing the solution:

- Analyst works with the application team to restore the configuration file to a known good state
- The restored configuration file is tested in a staging environment to ensure it resolves the performance issues
- Once validated, the configuration file is deployed to the production server, and the analyst monitors the server for any further issues

5. Documenting the incident and response process:

- Analyst creates a detailed incident report, outlining the timeline of events, root cause analysis, and remediation steps taken
- The report is shared with relevant stakeholders and stored in the organization's incident management system for future reference

SOLVING CONFIGURATION FILE ISSUES

C. Lessons learned and best practices

1. The importance of proactive monitoring and alerting:

- Implementing proactive monitoring and alerting mechanisms can help detect incidents early, minimizing their impact on the organization
- Regularly reviewing and tuning monitoring rules and thresholds can reduce false positives and improve incident detection accuracy

2. Collaboration and communication within the Blue Team:

- Effective collaboration and communication among SOC team members and other IT teams (application, network, and system administration) are crucial for efficient incident response
- Establishing clear roles, responsibilities, and communication channels can streamline the incident response process and ensure a coordinated effort

3. Continuous improvement and learning in defensive security:

- Regularly reviewing incident response processes and procedures to identify areas for improvement and incorporate lessons learned
- Encouraging SOC team members to pursue ongoing training and certifications to stay current with the latest defensive security techniques and best practices
- Participating in industry forums, conferences, and information-sharing groups to exchange knowledge and insights with peers

CHAPTER ELEVEN

Incident Response

CHAPTER ELEVEN
OBJECTIVES

After reading this chapter, the reader will be able to:

- Understand the key terms and concepts related to incident response, business continuity, and disaster recovery
- Identify the four main components of incident response and apply them to real-world scenarios
- Recognize the three possible models for incident response and determine which model best fits an organization's needs
- Develop a comprehensive Business Continuity Plan that includes essential components such as team members, immediate response procedures, notification systems, and management guidance
- Create a Disaster Recovery Plan that incorporates critical elements such as executive summaries, department-specific plans, technical guides, and checklists
- Communicate the importance of incident response, continuity, and resilience to stakeholders and advocate for the implementation of best practices within an organization

INCIDENT RESPONSE

A. Incident response key terms

- Incident: An event that compromises the confidentiality, integrity, or availability of an organization's systems, networks, or data
- Incident response: The process of detecting, investigating, containing, and recovering from a cybersecurity incident
- Incident response plan: A documented set of procedures and guidelines for handling cybersecurity incidents
- Incident response team: A group of individuals responsible for executing the incident response plan and managing the incident from detection to resolution

INCIDENT RESPONSE

B. Four main components of incident response

1. Preparation: Establishing an incident response plan, forming an incident response team, and acquiring the necessary tools and resources to handle incidents effectively

2. Detection and analysis: Identifying potential incidents through monitoring, alerts, and reports, and determining the nature, scope, and impact of the incident

3. Containment, eradication, and recovery: Isolating affected systems, removing malware and other threats, restoring systems to a secure state, and recovering data from backups

4. Post-incident activity: Conducting a thorough review of the incident, identifying lessons learned, updating incident response plans and security controls, and communicating with stakeholders

Example scenario: A SOC analyst detects unusual network traffic originating from a critical server. The incident response team is activated, and they begin investigating the incident. They determine that the server has been compromised by malware, and they quickly isolate the server to prevent further spread. The team then works to remove the malware, patch vulnerabilities, and restore the server from a clean backup. After the incident, they conduct a post-mortem review to identify the root cause and implement additional security measures to prevent similar incidents in the future.

INCIDENT RESPONSE

C. Three possible models for incident response

1. Internal incident response team: An organization maintains its own dedicated incident response team, consisting of employees with the necessary skills and expertise to handle incidents

2. Partially outsourced incident response: An organization maintains a small internal incident response team but also contracts with an external provider for additional support and resources during incidents

3. Fully outsourced incident response: An organization relies entirely on an external provider to handle incident response, often through a managed security service provider or specialized incident response firm

Example: A small financial services company decides to partially outsource its incident response function. They maintain a small internal team to handle minor incidents and coordinate with the external provider, while the external provider offers 24/7 monitoring, threat intelligence, and additional expertise for more complex incidents.

BUSINESS CONTINUITY PLANNING

A. Components of a BCP plan

A BCP plan is a comprehensive document that outlines how a business will continue operating during an unplanned disruption in services and should include the following components:

- Policy, purpose, and scope: This section outlines the reason for developing the BCP and the scope of the plan which defines the boundaries of the plan, specifying which business units, processes, systems, and facilities are covered
- Goals and objectives: This defines what the plan is trying to achieve.
- Key roles and responsibilities: This identifies who will be responsible for each function in the event of a disruption.
- Business impact analysis: This section identifies the critical business functions and the impact a disruption would have on them.
- Risk assessment: This determines the likelihood of various risks and the potential impact they would have on the business.
- Incident response: This outlines the immediate steps that should be taken when a disruption occurs.
- Recovery strategies: This outlines the strategies that will be used to recover critical business functions.
- Plan development and maintenance: This section outlines how the plan will be kept current and tested.

BUSINESS CONTINUITY PLANNING

B. BCP team members and contact information

The BCP plan should include a list of key team members and their contact information, such as:

- BCP coordinator: Responsible for overseeing the development, testing, and maintenance of the BCP plan
- Department representatives: Individuals from each critical business unit who are responsible for executing department-specific continuity procedures
- IT representatives: IT staff responsible for maintaining and recovering critical systems and infrastructure
- Executive sponsors: Senior leaders who provide oversight and support for the BCP program

Example contact list:

| Name | Role | Phone | Email |

| John Smith | BCP Coordinator | 555-123-4567 | john.smith@company.com |

| Sarah Johnson | Finance Representative | 555-987-6543 | sarah.johnson@company.com |

| Michael Lee | IT Manager | 555-246-8135 | michael.lee@company.com |

| Lisa Davis | Executive Sponsor | 555-369-2580 | lisa.davis@company.com |

BUSINESS CONTINUITY PLANNING

C. Immediate response procedures and checklists

The BCP plan should include clear, step-by-step procedures and checklists for immediate response actions, such as:

- Assessing the situation and determining the severity of the disruption
- Activating the BCP team and notifying key stakeholders
- Implementing alternate work arrangements, such as remote work or relocation to a backup site
- Communicating with employees, customers, and partners about the disruption and the organization's response

Example checklist:

[ ] Assess the situation and determine the scope of the disruption
[ ] Activate the BCP team and notify key stakeholders
[ ] Implement alternate work arrangements for critical functions
[ ] Communicate status updates to employees, customers, and partners
[ ] Monitor the situation and adjust response actions as needed

BUSINESS CONTINUITY PLANNING

D. Notification systems and call trees

The BCP plan should include a notification system and call tree to ensure that all relevant parties are informed of the disruption and the organization's response.

This may include:

- Mass notification systems: Automated systems that can quickly send messages to large groups via phone, email, or text message
- Call trees: A hierarchical communication structure where each person is responsible for contacting a specific group of individuals

Example call tree:

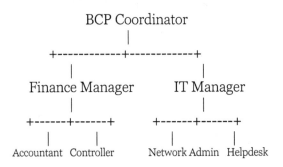

BUSINESS CONTINUITY PLANNING

E. Guidance for management and authority delegation

The BCP plan should provide guidance for management decision-making and authority delegation during a disruption, including:

- Criteria for activating and deactivating the BCP plan
- Roles and responsibilities of management team members
- Decision-making processes and escalation procedures
- Authority delegation and succession planning to ensure continuity of leadership

Example authority delegation table:

Role	Primary	Alternate
CEO	John Doe	Jane Smith
CFO	Sarah Johnson	Mark Davis
CIO	Michael Lee	Lisa Brown

BUSINESS CONTINUITY PLANNING

F. Enacting the BCP plan

When a disruption occurs, the organization should follow the procedures outlined in the BCP plan to enact the appropriate response and recovery actions.

This may include:

- Activating the BCP team and notifying stakeholders
- Implementing alternate work arrangements and workarounds
- Communicating with employees, customers, and partners
- Monitoring the situation and adjusting response actions as needed
- Coordinating with external parties, such as emergency responders or service providers

Example scenario: A severe weather event causes damage to an organization's primary office, rendering it unusable. The BCP coordinator activates the BCP plan and notifies the BCP team. Employees are instructed to work remotely using pre-established secure connections, while critical functions are relocated to a backup site. The organization communicates with customers and partners to inform them of the disruption and provide updates on service availability. The BCP team monitors the situation and adjusts response actions as needed until the primary office is restored and normal operations can resume.

BUSINESS CONTINUITY PLANNING

G. Critical supply chain contacts

The BCP plan should include contact information for critical suppliers, vendors, and partners who play a role in the organization's ability to maintain continuity during a disruption.

This may include:

- Utility providers (electricity, water, telecommunications)
- Hardware and software vendors
- Managed service providers
- Shipping and logistics partners

Example critical supplier contact list:

| Supplier | Service | Contact Name | Phone | Email |

| ABC Electric | Electricity | John Smith | 555-123-4567 | john.smith@abcelectric.com |

| XYZ Software | CRM System | Sarah Johnson | 555-987-6543 | sarah.johnson@xyzsoftware.com |

| 123 Shipping | Freight | Michael Lee | 555-246-8135 | michael.lee@123shipping.com |

DISASTER RECOVERY PLANNING

A. Five components to include in a DRP

A DRP is a documented process or set of procedures to recover and protect a business IT infrastructure in the event of a disaster.

1. Executive summary: A high-level overview of the DRP, including its purpose, scope, and key objectives

Example: "The purpose of this Disaster Recovery Plan is to ensure the timely restoration of critical IT systems and data in the event of a major disruption. The plan covers all essential IT infrastructure and services, and outlines the roles, responsibilities, and procedures for executing recovery operations."

2. Department-specific plans: Detailed recovery procedures and requirements for each critical business unit or department

Example:

- Finance Department Recovery Plan
- Critical Systems: Financial management system, payroll system, billing system
- Recovery Time Objective (RTO): 4 hours
- Recovery Point Objective (RPO): 1 hour

Recovery Procedures:

- Activate backup financial management system at secondary site
- Restore payroll data from latest backup
- Configure billing system to use secondary payment processor
- Notify finance team and provide access instructions

DISASTER RECOVERY PLANNING

3. Technical guides for IT personnel: Step-by-step instructions and technical documentation for recovering IT systems and infrastructure

Example:

Database Server Recovery Guide

1. Assess damage and determine recovery approach (restore from backup, failover to secondary server, etc.)

2. If restoring from backup:

- Mount latest backup from offsite storage
- Verify backup integrity and consistency
- Restore database to primary or secondary server

3. If failing over to secondary server:

- Verify secondary server is operational and in sync with primary
- Redirect traffic to secondary server
- Notify application owners and users of failover

4. Perform post-recovery testing and validation

5. Document recovery process and any issues encountered

DISASTER RECOVERY PLANNING

4. Full plan copies for disaster recovery team: Complete copies of the DRP, including all component plans and documentation, for each member of the disaster recovery team

Example:

"Each member of the disaster recovery team will be provided with a full copy of the DRP in both electronic and hard copy format. The electronic copy will be stored on a secure, encrypted USB drive, while the hard copy will be kept in a fireproof safe at the team member's home or office."

DISASTER RECOVERY PLANNING

5. Checklists for individuals: Quick reference guides and checklists for each team member, outlining their specific roles and responsibilities during a disaster recovery event

Example:

Database Administrator Recovery Checklist:

[ ] Assess damage and determine recovery approach
[ ] Coordinate with backup team to retrieve latest backups
[ ] Verify backup integrity and consistency
[ ] Restore databases to primary or secondary servers
[ ] Configure database connections and security settings
[ ] Perform post-recovery testing and validation
[ ] Document recovery process and any issues encountered
[ ] Participate in post-incident review and update recovery procedures as needed

CHAPTER TWELVE

Certification Pathways

CHAPTER TWELVE
OBJECTIVES

After reading this chapter, the reader will be able to:

- Identify the key cybersecurity certifications across various domains and vendors
- Understand the costs, prerequisites, and requirements associated with each certification
- Assess their current skills and experience to determine which certifications best align with their career goals
- Develop a strategic plan for preparing for and earning the chosen certifications
- Understand the importance of maintaining and renewing certifications through continuing education and professional development

KEY CYBERSECURITY CERTIFICATIONS

A. (ISC)² Certifications

1. Certified Information Systems Security Professional (CISSP)
- Cost: $749
- A globally recognized certification for experienced security professionals

2. Systems Security Certified Practitioner (SSCP)
- Cost: $249
- An entry-level certification focusing on hands-on technical skills and best practices

3. Certified Cloud Security Professional (CCSP)
- Cost: $599
- A certification focusing on cloud security architecture, design, operations, and service orchestration

4. Certified Authorization Professional (CAP)
- Cost: $599
- A certification focusing on the knowledge and skills needed to authorize and maintain information systems within the Risk Management Framework (RMF)

5. Certified in Cybersecurity (CC)
- Cost: Free
- A foundational certification that introduces core cybersecurity concepts and knowledge.

KEY CYBERSECURITY CERTIFICATIONS

6. Information Systems Security Architecture Professional (ISSAP)
- Cost: $599
- A concentration under CISSP that focuses on security architecture.

7. Certified in Governance, Risk, and Compliance (CGRC)
- Cost: $599
- A certification formerly known as CAP, focusing on governance and risk management.

8. Information Systems Security Engineering Professional (ISSEP)
- Cost: $599
- A CISSP concentration focusing on engineering aspects of security systems.

9. Certified Secure Software Lifecycle Professional (CSSLP)
- Cost: $599
- A certification focused on securing software development lifecycles.

10. Information Systems Security Management Professional (ISSMP)
- Cost: $599
- A CISSP concentration focusing on the management aspects of security programs.

KEY CYBERSECURITY CERTIFICATIONS

B. CompTIA Certifications

1. Security+
   - Cost: $381
   - An entry-level certification covering the essential principles of network security and risk management

2. CySA+
   - Cost: $359
   - An intermediate-level certification focusing on threat detection, incident response, and security architecture

3. PenTest+
   - Cost: $359
   - A certification focusing on penetration testing, vulnerability assessment, and management skills

4. Network+
   - Cost: $338
   - A foundational certification covering the essential skills needed to design, configure, manage, and troubleshoot wired and wireless networks

5. A+
   - Cost: $232 per exam (two exams required)
   - An entry-level certification validating the skills needed to support and troubleshoot computer hardware, software, and mobile devices

KEY CYBERSECURITY CERTIFICATIONS

6. Cloud+
   - Cost: $381
   - A certification focusing on cloud architecture, deployment, and automation.

7. Linux+
   - Cost: $358
   - A certification covering Linux operating system administration, security, and troubleshooting.

8. Server+
   - Cost: $338
   - A certification covering server architecture, storage, security, and troubleshooting.

9. CASP+
   - Cost: $494
   - An advanced-level certification focusing on enterprise security, risk management, and integration of computing systems.

10. Data+
    - Cost: $239
    - A certification focused on data management, analytics, and reporting.

KEY CYBERSECURITY CERTIFICATIONS

11. DataSys+
    - Cost: Varies
    - A specialized certification focusing on data systems administration and architecture.

12. DataX+
    - Cost: Varies
    - A certification focused on advanced data handling, storage, and processing techniques.

13. Project+
    - Cost: $358
    - A certification covering project management fundamentals, managing project life cycles, and ensuring timely delivery.

14. Cloud Essentials+
    - Cost: $123
    - An introductory certification covering the basics of cloud services, security, and business value.

KEY CYBERSECURITY CERTIFICATIONS

C. GIAC Certifications

1. GIAC Security Essentials
   - Cost: $2,499 for the certification attempt and two practice tests
   - A foundational certification covering the essential knowledge and skills required for hands-on security roles
   - Covers topics such as active defense, cryptography, incident handling, and network security

2. GIAC Certified Incident Handler
   - Cost: $2,499 for the certification attempt and two practice tests
   - A certification focusing on the skills needed to detect, respond to, and prevent cybersecurity incidents
   - Covers topics such as incident handling process, evidence acquisition and handling, and incident coordination and communication

3. GIAC Certified Intrusion Analyst
   - Cost: $2,499 for the certification attempt and two practice tests
   - A certification focusing on the skills needed to analyze and interpret network traffic and logs to identify and respond to intrusions
   - Covers topics such as network traffic analysis, IDS/IPS, and intrusion detection and prevention

KEY CYBERSECURITY CERTIFICATIONS

D. Offensive Security Certifications

1. Offensive Security Certified Professional
   - Cost: $999 for the course and certification attempt
   - A hands-on certification focusing on practical penetration testing skills and methodologies
   - Covers topics such as network enumeration, vulnerability scanning, web application attacks, and privilege escalation
   - Requires completion of the Penetration Testing with Kali Linux course and a 24-hour practical exam

2. Offensive Security Web Expert
   - Cost: $1,499 for the course and certification attempt
   - A hands-on certification focusing on advanced web application penetration testing skills
   - Covers topics such as web application assessment methodology, SQL injection, cross-site scripting, and authentication bypass
   - Requires completion of the Advanced Web Attacks and Exploitation course and a 48-hour practical exam

KEY CYBERSECURITY CERTIFICATIONS

E. Entry Level Cloud Security Certifications

1. AWS Certified Cloud Practitioner
   - Cost: $100
   - An entry-level certification covering the fundamentals of AWS Cloud and its services
   - Covers topics such as AWS Cloud concepts, security and compliance, technology, and billing and pricing

2. Microsoft Azure Fundamentals
   - Cost: $99
   - An entry-level certification covering the fundamentals of cloud services and how they are provided with Microsoft Azure
   - Covers topics such as cloud concepts, Azure services, Azure security and privacy, and Azure pricing and support

KEY CYBERSECURITY CERTIFICATIONS

3. Google Cloud Certified - Associate Cloud Engineer
   - Cost: $125
   - An entry-level certification validating the skills needed to deploy and manage applications on Google Cloud
   - Covers topics such as setting up cloud projects and accounts, deploying and monitoring cloud solutions, and managing access and security

4. Cloud Security Alliance Certificate of Cloud Security Knowledge (CCSK)
   - Cost: $395
   - A foundational certification covering the essential principles of cloud security
   - Covers topics such as cloud computing concepts, governance and enterprise risk management, legal issues and compliance, and data security

KEY CYBERSECURITY CERTIFICATIONS

F. Other Notable Certifications

1. Certified Ethical Hacker (CEH)
   - Cost: $1,199 for the course and certification attempt
   - A certification focusing on the skills needed to identify and exploit vulnerabilities in systems using the same tools and techniques as malicious hackers
   - Covers topics such as footprinting and reconnaissance, network scanning, enumeration, and hacking web applications

2. Certified Information Systems Auditor (CISA)
   - Cost: $575 for ISACA members, $760 for non-members
   - A certification focusing on the skills needed to audit, control, and monitor information systems
   - Covers topics such as the process of auditing information systems, governance and management of IT, and information systems acquisition, development, and implementation

3. Certified Information Security Manager (CISM)
   - Cost: $575 for ISACA members, $760 for non-members
   - A certification focusing on the skills needed to manage, design, and assess an enterprise's information security program
   - Covers topics such as information security governance, information risk management, information security program development and management, and information security incident management

CHOOSING THE RIGHT CERTIFICATION PATH

A. Assessing your current skills and experience

Before deciding on a certification path, it's crucial to assess your current skills and experience by considering the following factors:

- Assess your understanding of basic cybersecurity concepts, such as networking, operating systems, and security principles.
- While you may not have professional experience, consider any hands-on projects, labs, or exercises you've completed during your studies. These experiences can help you gauge your practical skills and identify areas for improvement.
- Investigate the learning resources available for the certifications you're considering. Many certifications offer official study guides, practice exams, and online courses. Assess whether these resources align with your learning style and if you have the time and discipline to commit to a self-study approach.
- Consider the costs associated with earning a certification, including exam fees, study materials, and any necessary training courses. Look for affordable options, such as bundled study packages or discounts for students. Some employers may also offer financial assistance for certification pursuits.
- Think about your long-term career aspirations in the cybersecurity field. Research different job roles and the certifications commonly required or preferred for those positions. This can help you choose a certification path that aligns with your goals and sets you up for success in your desired career track

CHOOSING THE RIGHT CERTIFICATION PATH

B. Defining your career goals and aspirations

Next, consider your long-term career goals and aspirations. Ask yourself:

- What type of cybersecurity role do you aspire to have in the future?
- What industries or sectors are you most interested in working in?
- What specific skills or knowledge do you want to acquire to advance your career?

CHOOSING THE RIGHT CERTIFICATION PATH

C. Researching the industry recognition and reputation of certifications

Not all certifications are created equal, and some may carry more weight or recognition within the industry than others. Research the reputation and recognition of the certifications you are considering by:

- Reviewing job postings and noting which certifications are frequently listed as requirements or preferences
- Engaging with professionals in your desired roles and asking for their opinions on the most valuable certifications
- Participating in online forums and communities to gather insights from other cybersecurity professionals

D. Evaluating the prerequisites and requirements for certifications

Certifications often have specific prerequisites and requirements that you must meet before you can earn the credential.

These may include:

- Minimum years of relevant work experience
- Completion of specific training courses
- Passing one or more exams
- Agreeing to a code of ethics or professional conduct

CHOOSING THE RIGHT CERTIFICATION PATH

E. Considering the costs and time commitment involved

Earning a cybersecurity certification can be a significant investment of both time and money.

Consider the following factors:

- Exam fees and any associated costs (study materials, training courses)
- Time required to study and prepare for the exam
- Potential travel costs if you need to take the exam at a testing center
- Opportunity cost of time spent studying (time away from work or other commitments)

PREPARING FOR CERTIFICATION EXAMS

A. Understanding the exam objectives and format

Before you start studying for a certification exam, make sure you thoroughly understand the exam objectives and format. Review the official certification website and any available exam guides to learn:

- The specific topics and domains covered on the exam
- The number and types of questions (multiple-choice, performance-based)
- The length of the exam and any time limits
- The passing score required to earn the certification

PREPARING FOR CERTIFICATION EXAMS

B. Studying with official resources and study materials

Most certification providers offer official study resources and materials to help you prepare for the exam.

These may include:

- Study guides and books
- Online training courses and webinars
- Practice exams and questions
- Hands-on labs and simulations

PREPARING FOR CERTIFICATION EXAMS

C. Practicing with hands-on labs and simulations

Many cybersecurity certifications, particularly those focused on technical skills, require hands-on experience and practical knowledge. To prepare for these exams, it's essential to practice with hands-on labs and simulations that replicate real-world scenarios.

Consider:

- Setting up a home lab environment to practice specific tools and techniques
- Completing virtual labs and simulations provided by the certification provider or third-party training companies
- Participating in capture-the-flag events or hacking challenges to test your skills in a competitive environment

D. Joining study groups and seeking mentorship

Preparing for a certification exam can be a lonely and daunting process, but you don't have to go it alone.

Consider:

- Joining online study groups or forums where you can connect with other professionals preparing for the same certification
- Seeking mentorship from experienced professionals who have already earned the certification you are pursuing

PREPARING FOR CERTIFICATION EXAMS

E. Taking practice exams and reviewing weak areas

As you near the end of your exam preparation, it's important to assess your readiness by taking practice exams and reviewing any weak areas. Many certification providers offer official practice exams that closely mirror the format and difficulty of the actual exam.

When reviewing your practice exam results, focus on:

- Identifying topics or domains where you struggled or scored poorly
- Reviewing the explanations for questions you answered incorrectly
- Adjusting your study plan to allocate more time and attention to your weak areas

MAINTAINING AND RENEWING CERTIFICATIONS

A. Understanding the continuing education requirements

Most cybersecurity certifications have ongoing continuing education requirements that you must meet to maintain your credential. These requirements ensure that you stay current with the latest industry developments and best practices.

Continuing education requirements may include:

- Earning a specified number of continuing education units or continuing professional education credits over a certain period
- Completing specific training courses or activities
- Participating in professional development events or conferences
- Contributing to the cybersecurity community through publications, presentations, or volunteer work

MAINTAINING AND RENEWING CERTIFICATIONS

B. Earning Continuing Professional Education credits

Continuing Professional Education credits are a common way to meet the continuing education requirements for cybersecurity certifications.

CPE credits can often be earned through a variety of activities, such as:

- Attending training courses, workshops, or webinars
- Participating in conferences or seminars
- Publishing articles, whitepapers, or blog posts
- Teaching or presenting on cybersecurity topics
- Volunteering for cybersecurity-related organizations or initiatives

MAINTAINING AND RENEWING CERTIFICATIONS

C. Staying updated with the latest industry trends and developments

The cybersecurity landscape is constantly evolving, with new threats, technologies, and best practices emerging regularly. To maintain your certification and stay effective in your role, it's crucial to stay updated with the latest industry trends and developments.

Some ways to do this include:

- Reading cybersecurity news sites, blogs, and publications
- Following thought leaders and influencers on social media
- Attending webinars, workshops, and conferences
- Participating in online forums and communities
- Pursuing additional certifications or training in emerging areas

MAINTAINING AND RENEWING CERTIFICATIONS

D. Participating in cybersecurity communities and events

Engaging with a cybersecurity community can be a valuable way to learn, network, and contribute to the collective knowledge of the field.

Consider:

- Joining professional organizations, such as ISACA, (ISC)^2, or ISSA
- Participating in local chapters or special interest groups related to your certification or area of expertise
- Attending conferences, workshops, or meetups to connect with other professionals and learn about the latest trends and best practices
- Engaging in online forums, discussion boards, or social media groups to share knowledge and collaborate with others in the field

MAINTAINING AND RENEWING CERTIFICATIONS

E. Contributing to the cybersecurity community through knowledge sharing

As you gain experience and expertise in your cybersecurity career, consider giving back to the community by sharing your knowledge and insights with others.

Some ways to contribute include:

- Writing articles, blog posts, or whitepapers on cybersecurity topics
- Presenting at conferences, webinars, or local meetups
- Mentoring or coaching aspiring cybersecurity professionals
- Participating in volunteer initiatives, such as developing cybersecurity awareness programs or supporting non-profit organizations

CHAPTER THIRTEEN

Skills Development

CHAPTER THIRTEEN
OBJECTIVES

After reading this chapter, the reader will be able to:

- Set up and manage virtual lab environments for practicing cybersecurity skills
- Conduct packet analysis using Wireshark to identify and analyze network traffic
- Perform system hardening and security configuration to reduce attack surfaces and improve security posture
- Configure and test firewall rules to control network access and mitigate potential threat
- Engage in CTF competitions and cyber ranges to further develop and refine cybersecurity skills
- Explore and utilize various open-source and commercial cybersecurity tools and resources for continuous learning and skill development

SETTING UP VIRTUAL LAB ENVIRONMENTS

A. Introduction to virtualization and its role in cybersecurity labs

Virtualization is the process of creating virtual versions of computer systems, networks, and resources, allowing multiple virtual environments to run on a single physical machine. In the context of cybersecurity labs, virtualization enables the creation of isolated, controlled environments for practicing various cybersecurity tasks and scenarios without impacting the host system or network.

B. Choosing the right virtualization platform

There are several popular virtualization platforms available, each with its own features and benefits. Two of the most widely used platforms are:

- VirtualBox: A free, open-source virtualization platform that supports multiple operating systems and offers a user-friendly interface for creating and managing virtual machines.
- VMware: A commercial virtualization platform that provides advanced features and performance, well-suited for enterprise-level virtualization needs. VMware offers a free version called VMware Workstation Player for personal, non-commercial use.

SETTING UP VIRTUAL LAB ENVIRONMENTS

C. Step-by-step guide to setting up a basic virtual lab

Here is a step-by-step guide to setting up a basic virtual lab using VirtualBox:

1. Download and install VirtualBox on your host system from the official website (https://www.virtualbox.org/).

2. Launch VirtualBox and click on the "New" button to create a new virtual machine.

3. Provide a name for the virtual machine, select the operating system and version, and allocate the appropriate amount of memory and storage.

4. Configure the virtual machine's network settings according to your lab requirements.

5. Install the desired operating system on the virtual machine using an ISO image or installation media.

6. Install any necessary tools, utilities, or vulnerable applications specific to your cybersecurity lab scenario.

7. Take a snapshot of the virtual machine to create a restore point, allowing you to easily revert to a clean state after each practice session.

SETTING UP VIRTUAL LAB ENVIRONMENTS

D. Best practices for managing and maintaining virtual labs

To ensure optimal performance and organization of your virtual labs, consider the following best practices:

- Allocate sufficient resources (memory, CPU, storage) to each virtual machine based on its purpose and requirements.
- Use descriptive names and labels for your virtual machines to easily identify their role and purpose.
- Regularly update and patch the host system and virtual machines to maintain security and stability.
- Use snapshots to create restore points before making significant changes or conducting potentially destructive tests.
- Regularly backup your virtual machines to protect against data loss and enable quick recovery in case of issues.
- Utilize shared folders or network shares to easily transfer files between the host system and virtual machines.
- Document the configuration, purpose, and any important notes for each virtual machine to facilitate effective management and collaboration.

PACKET ANALYSIS WITH WIRESHARK

A. Introduction to packet analysis and its importance in cybersecurity

Packet analysis is the process of capturing, inspecting, and interpreting network traffic data to understand network communication, identify potential security issues, and investigate incidents.

Packet analysis is essential for cybersecurity professionals to:

- Monitor network traffic for anomalies and suspicious activities
- Troubleshoot network connectivity and performance issues
- Detect and analyze network-based attacks, such as denial-of-service attacks or malware communication
- Investigate security incidents and gather evidence for forensic analysis
- Validate the effectiveness of security controls, such as firewalls and intrusion detection systems

PACKET ANALYSIS WITH WIRESHARK

B. Setting up the environment for packet analysis

To set up the environment for packet analysis using Wireshark, follow these steps:

1. Download and install Wireshark on your host system or a dedicated virtual machine from the official website (https://www.wireshark.org/).

2. Ensure that your network interface card supports promiscuous mode, which allows Wireshark to capture all network traffic, not just traffic addressed to your system.

3. Launch Wireshark and select the appropriate network interface to capture traffic from.

4. Start the packet capture and perform the desired network activity or scenario.

5. Stop the capture when the relevant traffic has been recorded.

PACKET ANALYSIS WITH WIRESHARK

C. Capturing and analyzing packets

Once the packet capture is complete, you can analyze the captured traffic using Wireshark's powerful features and filters:

- Browse the captured packets in the Packet List pane, which displays a summary of each packet, including source and destination addresses, protocols, and packet length.
- Select a packet of interest to view its details in the Packet Details pane, which shows the protocol hierarchy and the contents of each protocol layer.
- Use the display filters to focus on specific packets based on criteria such as protocol, IP address, or port number. For example, to view only HTTP traffic, enter "http" in the display filter bar.
- Analyze the packet details to identify relevant information, such as session establishment, data exchange, or error messages.
- Use Wireshark's built-in analysis tools, such as Expert Information, Protocol Hierarchy Statistics, and Conversations, to gain insights into the captured traffic.

PACKET ANALYSIS WITH WIRESHARK

D. Discussing the findings and potential mitigation strategies

After analyzing the captured packets, discuss your findings and potential mitigation strategies with your peers or instructor:

- Identify any notable or suspicious patterns, such as unusual protocols, port numbers, or payloads.
- Determine if the captured traffic indicates any security issues, such as unencrypted sensitive data, improper authentication, or communication with known malicious domains.
- Propose mitigation strategies based on your findings, such as implementing encryption, updating security policies, or blocking specific traffic using firewalls or IDS/IPS.
- Consider how the lessons learned from this packet analysis exercise can be applied to improve the overall security posture of an organization.

SYSTEM HARDENING AND SECURITY CONFIGURATION

A. Introduction to system hardening and its role in reducing attack surface

System hardening is the process of securing a system by reducing its attack surface and minimizing potential vulnerabilities. The goal of system hardening is to make it more difficult for attackers to compromise the system by:

- Removing or disabling unnecessary services, applications, and protocols
- Configuring secure settings for the operating system, applications, and network services
- Applying the principle of least privilege to user accounts and permissions
- Regularly updating and patching the system to address known vulnerabilities
- Implementing strong authentication and access controls

SYSTEM HARDENING AND SECURITY CONFIGURATION

B. Choosing a target system for hardening

For this practical activity, choose a target system that aligns with your learning goals and the systems commonly used in your desired cybersecurity domain.

Some popular options include:

1. Windows Server: A widely used server operating system in enterprise environments, offering various roles and features such as Active Directory, DNS, and IIS.

2. Linux: A family of open-source operating systems known for their stability, security, and flexibility, commonly used for servers, network devices, and security tools.

SYSTEM HARDENING AND SECURITY CONFIGURATION

C. Implementing system hardening techniques

Apply the following system hardening techniques to your chosen target system:

1. Disable unnecessary services and protocols:

- Windows: Use the Services console or PowerShell to identify and disable unneeded services.
- Linux: Use the systemctl or chkconfig utilities to list and disable unnecessary services.

2. Configure secure settings:

- Windows: Use Group Policy Objects or the Security Configuration Wizard to apply secure settings, such as password policies, account lockout, and audit policies.
- Linux: Modify configuration files (/etc/ssh/sshd_config, /etc/pam.d/common-password) to enforce secure settings, such as strong password requirements and SSH key-based authentication.

3. Apply the principle of least privilege:

- Windows: Use the Local Users and Groups manager or Active Directory to assign users to the appropriate groups and limit their permissions based on their roles.
- Linux: Use the useradd, usermod, and chmod commands to create users, assign them to groups, and set file and directory permissions.

SYSTEM HARDENING AND SECURITY CONFIGURATION

4. Update and patch the system:

- Windows: Use Windows Update or Windows Server Update Services to install the latest security patches and updates.
- Linux: Use the package manager (apt, yum) to update the system and install security patches.

5. Implement strong authentication and access controls:

- Windows: Enable and enforce multi-factor authentication using tools like Windows Hello or Azure MFA, and use Windows Firewall to control network access.
- Linux: Implement SSH key-based authentication, use sudo for privileged access, and configure iptables or nftables for network access control.

SYSTEM HARDENING AND SECURITY CONFIGURATION

D. Testing the hardened system's security posture

After implementing the hardening techniques, test the system's security posture to validate the effectiveness of the applied controls:

- Conduct vulnerability scans using tools like Nessus, OpenVAS, or Microsoft Baseline Security Analyzer to identify any remaining vulnerabilities or misconfigurations.
- Perform penetration testing to simulate real-world attacks and attempt to exploit any weaknesses in the system's defenses.
- Review system logs and monitoring tools to detect any suspicious activities or unauthorized access attempts.
- Assess the system's compliance with relevant security standards and benchmarks.

SYSTEM HARDENING AND SECURITY CONFIGURATION

E. Documenting the hardening process and lessons learned

Document the system hardening process and the lessons learned to create a valuable reference for future projects and to share knowledge with others:

- Record the specific hardening techniques applied, including the steps taken and the tools used.
- Note any challenges or obstacles encountered during the process and how they were overcome.
- Summarize the results of the security posture testing and any remaining risks or areas for improvement.
- Reflect on the key takeaways from the activity and how they can be applied to real-world scenarios.

CONFIGURING AND TESTING FIREWALL RULES

A. Introduction to firewalls and their role in network security

Firewalls are security devices or software that monitor and control incoming and outgoing network traffic based on predetermined security rules. Firewalls play a critical role in network security by:

- Establishing a barrier between trusted internal networks and untrusted external networks, such as the Internet
- Enforcing network access controls based on IP addresses, port numbers, protocols, and application-level data
- Preventing unauthorized access, malware propagation, and other network-based threats
- Logging and auditing network traffic for security analysis and compliance purposes

CONFIGURING AND TESTING FIREWALL RULES

B. Setting up a virtual network with a firewall appliance

To practice configuring and testing firewall rules, set up a virtual network using a firewall appliance like pfSense:

1. Download the pfSense ISO image from the official website (https://www.pfsense.org/).

2. Create a new virtual machine in your virtualization platform (VirtualBox, VMware) and attach the pfSense ISO image to the virtual machine's optical drive.

3. Configure the virtual machine's network adapters to create a multi-segment network, such as:
- WAN (eth0): Connected to the host system's network or a virtual NAT network for Internet access.
- LAN (eth1): Connected to an internal virtual network switch for the trusted local network.
- OPT1 (eth2): Connected to another internal virtual network switch for a DMZ or guest network.

4. Install and configure pfSense on the virtual machine following the prompts and best practices.

5. Access the pfSense web interface using a web browser on a client machine connected to the LAN network.

CONFIGURING AND TESTING FIREWALL RULES

C. Configuring firewall rules

Configure firewall rules in pfSense to control network access and enforce security policies:

1. Navigate to the "Firewall > Rules" menu in the pfSense web interface.

2. Select the appropriate interface tab (WAN, LAN, OPT1) for the rule you want to create.

3. Click the "Add" button to create a new firewall rule.

4. Configure the rule settings, such as:
- Action: Choose "Pass" to allow traffic or "Block" to deny traffic.
- Interface: Select the interface the rule applies to (WAN, LAN, OPT1).
- Protocol: Specify the protocol (TCP, UDP, ICMP) or select "Any" for all protocols.
- Source: Define the source IP address, network, or alias for the traffic.
- Destination: Specify the destination IP address, network, or alias for the traffic.
- Destination port range: Define the destination port range for the traffic (80 for HTTP, 443 for HTTPS).
- Description: Add a brief description of the rule's purpose for better organization and management.

Save the rule and apply the changes.

CONFIGURING AND TESTING FIREWALL RULES

D. Testing the firewall configuration

Test the firewall configuration to ensure that the rules are working as intended and that the network is properly secured:

- Use a client machine connected to the LAN network to attempt to access resources and services as defined by the firewall rules.
- Test both allowed and blocked scenarios to confirm that the rules are being enforced correctly.
- Use network scanning tools, such as Nmap, to probe the firewall from the WAN side and identify any open ports or services that should be blocked.
- Perform penetration testing to simulate real-world attacks and attempt to bypass the firewall rules.
- Verify that the firewall is properly logging traffic and security events for analysis and auditing purposes.

CONFIGURING AND TESTING FIREWALL RULES

E. Analyzing the firewall logs for security events and potential improvements

Regularly analyze the firewall logs to identify security events and potential areas for improvement:

- Use the pfSense web interface to access the firewall logs (Status > System Logs > Firewall).
- Review the logs for blocked traffic, suspicious connection attempts, and other notable events.
- Look for patterns or trends in the logged events that may indicate ongoing attacks, misconfigured rules, or other security issues.
- Use log analysis tools or a SIEM solution to correlate firewall events with other security logs and gain a more comprehensive view of the network's security posture.
- Based on the log analysis findings, consider adjusting firewall rules, implementing additional security controls, or updating the organization's security policies and procedures.

MINI PROJECTS AND CHALLENGES

A. Introduction to Capture the Flag competitions and cyber ranges

Capture the Flag competitions and cyber ranges are interactive, hands-on learning environments that challenge participants to solve cybersecurity problems and test their skills in realistic scenarios. These platforms are designed to help individuals and teams develop practical experience, critical thinking, and problem-solving abilities in a fun and engaging way.

CTF competitions typically involve a series of challenges or puzzles that participants must solve to obtain "flags" or unique strings of text that demonstrate their successful completion of each task. These challenges can cover a wide range of cybersecurity topics, such as cryptography, web application security, reverse engineering, and network forensics.

Cyber ranges are virtualized environments that simulate real-world networks and systems, allowing participants to practice offensive and defensive cybersecurity techniques in a safe and controlled setting. Cyber ranges often include a variety of target systems, such as vulnerable web applications, misconfigured servers, and simulated industrial control systems, which participants must assess, secure, or exploit depending on their role (red team or blue team).

MINI PROJECTS AND CHALLENGES

B. Benefits of participating in CTFs and cyber ranges

Participating in CTF competitions and cyber ranges offers numerous benefits for aspiring cybersecurity professionals:

- CTFs and cyber ranges provide practical, hands-on experience with real-world cybersecurity tools, techniques, and scenarios, allowing participants to apply their knowledge and develop their skills in a practical setting.
- These platforms cover a wide range of cybersecurity topics and technologies, exposing participants to new concepts, tools, and techniques that they may not encounter in their daily work or studies.
- CTFs and cyber ranges challenge participants to think creatively, analyze complex problems, and develop innovative solutions under time pressure, helping to build critical thinking and problem-solving skills that are essential in the field of cybersecurity.
- Many CTFs and cyber range exercises are designed to be completed in teams, fostering collaboration, communication, and teamwork skills that are crucial in real-world cybersecurity roles.
- Participating in CTFs and cyber ranges provides opportunities to connect with other cybersecurity enthusiasts, professionals, and experts, building valuable relationships and expanding one's professional network.
- Demonstrating participation and success in CTFs and cyber ranges can be a valuable addition to a cybersecurity professional's resume, showcasing their practical skills, dedication to continuous learning, and ability to perform under pressure.

MINI PROJECTS AND CHALLENGES

C. Examples of popular CTF platforms and cyber ranges

1. Hack The Box

Hack The Box is a popular online platform that offers a wide variety of CTF-style challenges and simulated environments for practicing offensive and defensive cybersecurity skills. The platform features a range of difficulty levels, from beginner to expert, and covers topics such as penetration testing, reverse engineering, and cryptography. Hack The Box also offers a competitive ranking system, allowing participants to earn points and climb the leaderboard based on their performance.

2. TryHackMe

TryHackMe is an online learning platform that offers guided learning paths and hands-on labs for various cybersecurity topics. It provides a structured approach to learning, with interactive lessons and challenges that cover topics like network security, web application security, and penetration testing. TryHackMe is beginner-friendly and offers a supportive community for learners.

MINI PROJECTS AND CHALLENGES

3. VulnHub

VulnHub is a platform that provides a collection of intentionally vulnerable virtual machines for users to practice their offensive cybersecurity skills. These virtual machines are designed to simulate real-world vulnerabilities and misconfigurations, allowing participants to develop their penetration testing and ethical hacking abilities in a legal and controlled environment. VulnHub challenges are often used as a preparation tool for aspiring penetration testers and security researchers.

4. SANS Cyber Ranges

SANS Institute, a well-known provider of cybersecurity training and certification, offers cyber ranges that simulate realistic network environments and security scenarios. These ranges are designed to help individuals and teams develop practical skills in areas such as incident response, digital forensics, and industrial control system security. SANS Cyber Ranges often include a combination of lecture-style instruction and hands-on exercises, providing a comprehensive learning experience for participants.

MINI PROJECTS AND CHALLENGES

D. Tips for success in CTFs and cyber ranges

To make the most of your participation in CTFs and cyber ranges, consider the following tips:

- If you are new to CTFs or cyber ranges, begin with beginner-friendly challenges or guided learning paths to build a strong foundation in core cybersecurity concepts and techniques.
- While it can be tempting to focus solely on solving challenges and earning points, remember that the primary goal is to learn and develop your skills. Take the time to understand the underlying concepts and techniques behind each challenge, and don't be afraid to ask for help or explanations when needed.
- Many CTFs and cyber ranges are designed to be completed in teams, so embrace the opportunity to collaborate with others and learn from their perspectives and experiences. Share your knowledge and insights with your teammates, and be open to feedback and suggestions.
- Keep a record of the challenges you complete, the tools and techniques you use, and the lessons you learn along the way. This documentation can serve as a valuable reference for future challenges and real-world scenarios, and can also be used to demonstrate your skills and experience to potential employers.
- Make a habit of dedicating time each week or month to practicing on these platforms, and seek out new challenges and opportunities to push yourself outside of your comfort zone.
- Many CTF platforms and cyber ranges have active communities of participants and organizers who share resources, tips, and insights.
- As you develop your skills through CTFs and cyber ranges, look for opportunities to apply what you've learned to real-world situations, such as securing your own home network, contributing to open-source security projects, or participating in bug bounty programs.

EXPLORING CYBERSECURITY TOOLS AND RESOURCES

A. Open-source tools for various security tasks

1. Network scanning and enumeration

Network Mapper is a popular open-source tool used for network discovery, port scanning, and service enumeration. It allows cybersecurity professionals to identify active hosts, open ports, and running services on a network, which is essential for assessing the attack surface and identifying potential vulnerabilities. Nmap supports a wide range of scanning techniques and can be used for both offensive and defensive purposes, such as penetration testing and network auditing.

2. Vulnerability assessment

Open Vulnerability Assessment System is a free and open-source vulnerability scanner that helps identify security weaknesses in systems, networks, and applications. It consists of a scanner engine, a regularly updated feed of Network Vulnerability Tests, and a web-based management interface. OpenVAS can be used to perform automated vulnerability scans, generate reports, and integrate with other security tools for a more comprehensive vulnerability management process.

EXPLORING CYBERSECURITY TOOLS AND RESOURCES

3. Web application testing

OWASP ZAP is an open-source web application security scanner developed by the Open Web Application Security Project. It is designed to help cybersecurity professionals find vulnerabilities in web applications through automated scanning and manual testing. OWASP ZAP includes features like intercepting proxy, automated scanners, fuzzing, and scripting support, making it a versatile tool for identifying and exploiting web application vulnerabilities.

4. Incident response and forensics

Volatility is an open-source memory forensics framework that allows cybersecurity professionals to analyze memory dumps from various operating systems, including Windows, Linux, and macOS. It provides a set of tools and plugins for extracting digital artifacts from memory dumps, such as running processes, network connections, and cached files. Volatility is widely used in incident response and digital forensics investigations to identify malware, reconstruct past events, and gather evidence.

EXPLORING CYBERSECURITY TOOLS AND RESOURCES

B. Commercial cybersecurity tools and platforms

1. Security information and event management solutions

SIEM solutions collect, analyze, and correlate log data from various sources across an organization's network to detect security threats and anomalies in real-time. They provide a centralized platform for security monitoring, incident detection, and compliance reporting. Popular commercial SIEM solutions include Splunk, IBM QRadar, and LogRhythm.

2. Endpoint detection and response platforms

EDR platforms monitor and collect data from endpoints (workstations, servers, mobile devices) to detect, investigate, and respond to advanced threats and malicious activities. They provide capabilities like real-time monitoring, behavioral analysis, threat hunting, and automated response actions. Leading commercial EDR solutions include CrowdStrike Falcon, Carbon Black, and SentinelOne.

3. Penetration testing and vulnerability management tools

Commercial penetration testing and vulnerability management tools offer advanced features and enterprise-level support for organizations looking to assess and improve their security posture. These tools often include automated scanning, reporting, and integration capabilities, as well as expert guidance and support. Examples of popular commercial tools in this category include Rapid7 InsightVM, Tenable Nessus, and Acunetix.

EXPLORING CYBERSECURITY TOOLS AND RESOURCES

C. Online resources and communities for continuous learning

1. Cybersecurity blogs and news sites

Staying updated with the latest cybersecurity trends, threats, and best practices is crucial for professionals in the field. Cybersecurity blogs and news sites provide valuable insights, tutorials, and expert opinions.

Some popular resources include:

- Krebs on Security: In-depth investigative journalism and analysis of cybercrime and cybersecurity issues, authored by Brian Krebs.
- Dark Reading: A comprehensive source for cybersecurity news, analysis, and opinion, covering topics like threats, vulnerabilities, and industry trends.
- Threatpost: An independent news site that focuses on providing the latest information and analysis on cybersecurity threats, vulnerabilities, and attacks.
- The Hacker News: A popular cybersecurity news platform that covers a wide range of topics, including cyber attacks, data breaches, and security research.

EXPLORING CYBERSECURITY TOOLS AND RESOURCES

2. Online courses and training platforms

Online learning platforms offer a wealth of cybersecurity courses and training programs for professionals at all skill levels.

Some popular platforms include:

- Cybrary: A free online learning community that offers courses, labs, and assessments on various cybersecurity topics, as well as certification preparation materials.
- SANS: A well-respected provider of cybersecurity training and certification, offering both online and in-person courses taught by industry experts.
- Coursera: An online learning platform that partners with top universities and organizations to offer courses and specializations in cybersecurity and related fields.
- Udemy: A large online learning marketplace that features a wide selection of cybersecurity courses created by individual instructors and industry professionals.

EXPLORING CYBERSECURITY TOOLS AND RESOURCES

3. Professional networks and forums

Engaging with the cybersecurity community through professional networks and forums is an excellent way to learn from experts, share knowledge, and collaborate on projects.

Some popular platforms include:

- LinkedIn: The world's largest professional networking site, where professionals can connect, share insights, and find job opportunities.
- Reddit: A popular social news aggregation and discussion platform, with subreddits like r/netsec, r/cybersecurity, and r/netsecstudents, where users can ask questions, share resources, and engage in technical discussions related to cybersecurity.
- Discord: A communication platform that hosts various cybersecurity-related servers, allowing professionals to chat, share resources, and collaborate in real-time.

CHAPTER FOURTEEN

Professional Skills

CHAPTER FOURTEEN
OBJECTIVES

After reading this chapter, the reader will be able to:

- Understand the importance of fundamental skills, such as networking, pentesting, and incident handling, in the context of cybersecurity professional development
- Identify and cultivate the essential traits, including problem-solving, communication, adaptability, and ethical behavior, that are crucial for success in the field
- Engage with the cybersecurity community and stay updated with the latest trends, threats, and best practices
- Build a compelling portfolio of experience that showcases their skills and practical expertise
- Develop and demonstrate strong technical writing, documentation, and presentation abilities to effectively communicate with various audiences
- Embrace a mindset of continuous learning and skill advancement to stay relevant and competitive in the ever-changing landscape of cybersecurity

TOP FUNDAMENTAL SKILLS

A. Networking at Packet Level

1. Understanding TCP/IP, switching, routing, firewalls, and load balancing

A solid grasp of networking concepts is essential for cybersecurity professionals. This includes understanding the TCP/IP model, which defines how data is encapsulated and transmitted across networks, as well as the roles of switches, routers, firewalls, and load balancers in managing and securing network traffic. Familiarity with protocols like IP, TCP, UDP, and ICMP, and their associated port numbers, is crucial for analyzing network behavior and identifying potential threats.

2. Mastering command line tools for network analysis and troubleshooting

Proficiency in using command line tools is a must-have skill for cybersecurity professionals. Tools like ping, traceroute, nslookup, and netstat allow for quick and efficient network analysis and troubleshooting. For example, using ping to test connectivity, traceroute to map network paths, nslookup to query DNS records, and netstat to view active network connections. Mastering these tools enables professionals to diagnose issues, investigate suspicious activities, and gather critical information during incident response.

TOP FUNDAMENTAL SKILLS

B. Pentesting and Reverse Engineering

1. Developing expertise in identifying and exploiting vulnerabilities

Penetration testing, or ethical hacking, is a core skill for cybersecurity professionals. It involves proactively identifying vulnerabilities in systems, networks, and applications, and safely exploiting them to assess the potential impact of a breach. This requires a deep understanding of various attack vectors, such as SQL injection, cross-site scripting, and buffer overflow, as well as the ability to think like an attacker and anticipate their moves. Developing expertise in vulnerability assessment tools, like Nmap and Nessus, and staying updated with the latest exploit techniques is essential for effective pentesting.

2. Building a toolbox for effective penetration testing and reverse engineering

To be successful in pentesting and reverse engineering, cybersecurity professionals need to build a diverse toolbox of software and utilities. This may include tools for reconnaissance (eRecon-ng, theHarvester), vulnerability scanning (Burp Suite, Metasploit), password cracking (John the Ripper, Hashcat), and binary analysis (IDA Pro, Ghidra). Familiarity with scripting languages like Python and Bash is also valuable for automating tasks and developing custom exploits. By curating a well-rounded toolbox, professionals can adapt to various pentesting scenarios and efficiently identify and exploit vulnerabilities.

TOP FUNDAMENTAL SKILLS

C. Navigating the InfoSec Community

1. Engaging with the cybersecurity community through forums, conferences, and networking events

Active participation in the cybersecurity community is crucial for professional growth and staying current with industry developments. Engaging in online forums allows professionals to ask questions, share knowledge, and learn from experienced practitioners. Attending conferences like DEF CON, Black Hat, and RSA Conference provides opportunities to hear from industry leaders, explore cutting-edge research, and network with peers. Local meetups and hackathons are also valuable for building relationships and collaborating on projects.

2. Staying updated with the latest trends, threats, and best practices

To stay ahead of the curve, professionals must make a habit of continuously learning and staying informed. This can be achieved by following reputable cybersecurity blogs and news sources, such as Krebs on Security, Threatpost, and Dark Reading, as well as subscribing to industry newsletters and podcasts. Regularly reading research papers, whitepapers, and vendor reports helps professionals gain insights into the latest attack techniques, vulnerabilities, and mitigation measures.

TOP FUNDAMENTAL SKILLS

D. Building a Portfolio of Experience

1. Documenting projects, certifications, and contributions to showcase skills

A strong portfolio is essential for demonstrating practical experience and expertise to potential employers and colleagues. Cybersecurity professionals should make a habit of documenting their projects, including the tools and techniques used, the challenges encountered, and the outcomes achieved. This can include write-ups of CTF challenges, blog posts about new tools or techniques, or GitHub repositories showcasing scripts and code samples. Earning relevant certifications and highlighting them in the portfolio further validates a professional's skills and dedication to the field.

2. Demonstrating practical experience through lab environments, CTFs, and real-world scenarios

Hands-on experience is the key to developing and refining cybersecurity skills. Setting up personal lab environments, using platforms like VirtualBox or AWS, allows professionals to safely experiment with different tools and techniques, and practice responding to simulated threats. Participating in CTF competitions and online challenges, such as those offered by Hack The Box and VulnHub, helps professionals sharpen their problem-solving abilities and gain exposure to real-world scenarios. Contributing to open-source security projects or volunteering for local organizations are also excellent ways to gain practical experience and make a positive impact in the community.

TOP FUNDAMENTAL SKILLS

E. Incident Handling

1. Developing a systematic approach to incident response and forensics

Effective incident handling requires a structured and methodical approach. Cybersecurity professionals should be well-versed in the incident response lifecycle, which includes preparation, detection and analysis, containment, eradication, recovery, and lessons learned. This involves developing and testing incident response plans, establishing clear communication channels and escalation procedures, and maintaining detailed documentation throughout the process. Familiarity with forensic techniques, such as disk imaging, memory analysis, and log analysis, is crucial for investigating incidents and gathering evidence.

2. Collaborating with teams to effectively contain, eradicate, and recover from security incidents

Incident response is a team effort, requiring close collaboration between cybersecurity professionals, IT staff, legal counsel, and executive leadership. Effective communication and coordination are essential for quickly containing and mitigating the impact of a security incident. This may involve working with network administrators to isolate affected systems, coordinating with PR teams to manage public disclosure, and liaising with law enforcement agencies in cases of criminal activity. Building strong relationships and fostering a culture of collaboration and trust are key to successful incident handling.

ESSENTIAL CYBERSECURITY TRAITS

A. Problem-Solving and Critical Thinking

1. Cultivating analytical abilities to identify and solve complex security challenges

Cybersecurity professionals face a constant stream of complex problems and challenges that require strong analytical and problem-solving skills. This involves breaking down complex issues into smaller, manageable components, gathering and evaluating relevant information, and applying logical reasoning to identify the root cause of a problem. Professionals should cultivate a curious and inquisitive mindset, asking probing questions and challenging assumptions to gain a deeper understanding of the issues at hand.

2. Gathering facts, analyzing information, and making informed decisions

Effective problem-solving in cybersecurity requires a data-driven approach. Professionals must be skilled at gathering and analyzing information from various sources, such as logs, network traffic, and threat intelligence feeds, to paint a comprehensive picture of a security incident or vulnerability. This involves using statistical analysis and data visualization tools to identify patterns, anomalies, and trends, and drawing insights to inform decision-making. Professionals should also be comfortable using their best judgment to make decisions based on available information and potential risks.

ESSENTIAL CYBERSECURITY TRAITS

B. Communication and Collaboration

1. Developing strong written and verbal communication skills

Cybersecurity professionals must be able to communicate complex technical concepts and ideas to both technical and non-technical audiences. This requires strong written and verbal communication skills, including the ability to explain technical details in clear, concise, and accessible language. Professionals should be comfortable creating a variety of written materials, such as incident reports, policy documents, and user guides, tailoring the content and style to the intended audience. Verbal communication skills are equally important, whether presenting findings to executives, conducting security awareness training, or collaborating with cross-functional teams.

2. Working effectively in teams, fostering collaboration, and resolving conflicts

Cybersecurity is a highly collaborative field, requiring professionals to work closely with colleagues from various departments and backgrounds. Effective teamwork involves actively listening to others' ideas and concerns, providing constructive feedback, and fostering an inclusive and respectful work environment. Professionals should be skilled at building relationships, establishing trust, and finding common ground to achieve shared goals. When conflicts arise, they must be able to navigate difficult conversations, find compromises, and maintain a focus on the overall objectives of the team and organization.

ESSENTIAL CYBERSECURITY TRAITS

C. Adaptability and Persistence

1. Embracing change and adapting to new technologies and evolving threats

Professionals must be adaptable and open to change, embracing new tools, techniques, and approaches as they become available. This requires a willingness to learn and experiment, stepping outside of one's comfort zone to explore unfamiliar areas and expand one's skill set. Adaptability also involves being proactive in anticipating and preparing for future challenges, such as the security implications of AI and machine learning.

2. Demonstrating persistence and dedication in the face of challenges

Cybersecurity professionals often face complex and seemingly intractable problems, from vulnerabilities to sophisticated cyber attacks. Persistence and dedication are essential traits for success in this field, as professionals must be willing to put in the time and effort required to find solutions and see projects through to completion. This may involve long hours of research, trial and error, and troubleshooting, as well as the resilience to bounce back from setbacks and learn from failures. Maintaining a passion for the work and a commitment to the larger mission of protecting individuals and organizations from cyber threats can help professionals stay motivated and focused in the face of challenges.

ESSENTIAL CYBERSECURITY TRAITS

D. Attention to Detail and Responsibility

1. Maintaining a cautious approach to security tasks and documentation

Attention to detail is critical in cybersecurity, as even small oversights or misconfigurations can have significant consequences. Professionals must be cautious in their approach to security tasks, double-checking their work and ensuring that all steps are followed correctly and completely. This includes carefully reviewing code for potential vulnerabilities, thoroughly testing security controls before deployment, and maintaining accurate and up-to-date documentation of systems, policies, and procedures. Professionals should also be proactive in identifying and addressing potential risks and issues before they become major problems.

2. Taking ownership of actions and being accountable for results

Cybersecurity professionals have a great deal of responsibility, as their actions can directly impact the security and privacy of individuals and organizations. As such, they must be willing to take ownership of their work and be accountable for the results. This involves being transparent about potential risks and limitations, communicating regularly with stakeholders, and taking prompt action to address any issues or concerns that arise. Professionals should also be proactive in seeking feedback and input from others, and be willing to admit and learn from mistakes.

ESSENTIAL CYBERSECURITY TRAITS

E. Ethical Mindset

1. Upholding integrity and adhering to ethical principles in cybersecurity practice

Cybersecurity professionals have access to sensitive information and powerful tools that can be used for both good and ill. As such, it is essential that they uphold the highest standards of integrity and ethics in their work. This involves adhering to established codes of conduct, such as the (ISC)² Code of Ethics, and always acting in the best interests of their organizations and the wider public. Professionals must be transparent about their actions and motivations, avoid conflicts of interest, and respect the privacy and confidentiality of the data they handle. They should also be willing to speak up and report unethical or illegal behavior, even if it means challenging the actions of colleagues or superiors.

2. Respecting privacy, confidentiality, and the responsible disclosure of vulnerabilities

Cybersecurity professionals have a responsibility to protect the privacy and confidentiality of the individuals and organizations they serve. This involves handling sensitive data with care, using appropriate safeguards and access controls, and only sharing information on a need-to-know basis. When vulnerabilities are discovered, professionals must follow responsible disclosure practices, notifying affected parties and giving them adequate time to develop and deploy patches before publicly releasing details. Professionals should also be mindful of the potential impacts of their work, considering the ethical implications of their actions and striving to minimize harm and promote the greater good.

DEVELOPING AND SHOWCASING SKILLS

A. Technical Writing and Documentation

1. Crafting clear and concise technical reports, policies, and procedures

Effective technical writing is a key skill for cybersecurity professionals, as they must be able to communicate complex information in a clear and accessible manner. This involves creating well-structured and logically organized documents, using simple and direct language, and avoiding jargon and technical terms where possible. Professionals should be skilled at writing a variety of technical documents, such as incident reports, policy recommendations, and standard operating procedures, tailoring the content and style to the intended audience. Attention to detail is critical, as even small errors or uncertainty can lead to confusion or misinterpretation.

2. Maintaining accurate and up-to-date documentation for security projects and incidents

Accurate and up-to-date documentation is essential for effective cybersecurity management and incident response. Professionals should make a habit of regularly documenting their work, including the tools and techniques used, the steps taken, and the outcomes achieved. This may include creating network diagrams, asset inventories, and configuration files, as well as maintaining detailed logs of security events and investigations. By keeping thorough and organized records, professionals can ensure that critical information is readily available when needed, and that lessons learned from past incidents are captured and applied to future efforts.

DEVELOPING AND
SHOWCASING SKILLS

B. Presentation and Awareness

1. Creating engaging and informative cybersecurity awareness materials

One of the most effective ways to improve an organization's security posture is to raise awareness and understanding among employees and stakeholders. Cybersecurity professionals should be skilled at creating engaging and informative awareness materials, such as presentations, posters, and videos, that convey key security concepts and best practices in a simple and memorable way. This may involve using storytelling techniques, visual aids, and real-world examples to make the content more relatable and impactful. Professionals should also be mindful of the different learning styles and preferences of their audience, using a variety of formats and channels to reach the widest possible audience.

2. Delivering effective presentations to technical and non-technical audiences

Cybersecurity professionals are often called upon to present their findings and recommendations to a wide range of audiences, from technical teams to executive leadership. Effective presentation skills are essential for communicating complex information in a clear and persuasive manner, and for building support and buy-in for security initiatives. Professionals should be comfortable with public speaking, using appropriate body language and vocal techniques to engage and connect with their audience. They should also be skilled at creating visually appealing and well-organized slide decks, using graphics and other visual aids to clarify and reinforce key points.

DEVELOPING AND SHOWCASING SKILLS

C. Continuous Learning and Skill Advancement

1. Staying curious and committed to learning new skills and technologies

To stay relevant and effective, professionals must be committed to continuous learning and skill development. This involves staying curious and proactive, seeking out new information and opportunities to expand one's knowledge and expertise. Professionals should make a habit of reading industry publications, attending conferences and webinars, and participating in online forums and communities to stay up-to-date with the latest developments. They should also be willing to experiment with new tools and techniques, and to take on new challenges and responsibilities that stretch their abilities and broaden their horizons.

2. Pursuing relevant certifications and participating in training programs

In addition to self-directed learning, pursuing formal certifications and training programs can be a valuable way for cybersecurity professionals to demonstrate their skills and advance their careers. Many employers require or prefer candidates with specific certifications as they provide a standardized benchmark of knowledge and expertise. Participating in training programs, such as those offered by SANS Institute or Offensive Security, can also help professionals gain hands-on experience with the latest tools and techniques, and network with other practitioners in the field. When selecting certifications or training programs, professionals should consider their career goals, current skill level, and the specific requirements of their industry or organization.

CHAPTER FIFTEEN

Career Accelerator

CHAPTER FIFTEEN
OBJECTIVES

After reading this chapter, the reader will be able to:

- Craft a compelling technical resume and cover letter that showcases their skills and experience
- Optimize their LinkedIn and Handshake profiles to attract potential employers and networking opportunities
- Research and target top cybersecurity companies and roles that align with their interests and qualifications
- Prepare effectively for cybersecurity interviews, including developing a strong narrative and addressing common questions
- Assess their skills and interests to choose the right cybersecurity career path
- Utilize job search strategies and resources to find and apply for relevant cybersecurity positions
- Negotiate job offers and compensation packages to ensure fair and competitive terms
- Develop a customized career action plan with clear goals, timelines, and milestones
- Overcome common obstacles, such as imposter syndrome and job search challenges, and maintain motivation throughout their career journey

BUILDING A STRONG PROFESSIONAL PROFILE

A. Crafting a Technical Resume

A well-crafted technical resume is essential for showcasing your skills, experience, and qualifications to potential employers in the cybersecurity field.

Reasons to write a technical resume:

- A technical resume allows you to highlight your proficiency in specific technologies, tools, and programming languages that are relevant to the job you are applying for. It demonstrates your depth of knowledge and hands-on experience in your field of expertise.
- Technical roles often require strong problem-solving abilities. By including examples of complex technical challenges you have overcome or projects you have successfully completed, you can showcase your ability to analyze problems, develop innovative solutions, and deliver results.
- A technical resume provides an opportunity to emphasize your notable technical accomplishments, such as developing a new software application, optimizing network performance, or implementing robust security measures. These achievements demonstrate your ability to apply your technical skills effectively and make a tangible impact.
- By customizing your technical resume to align with the specific requirements of the job posting, you can demonstrate that you possess the exact skills and experience the employer is seeking. This targeted approach increases your chances of capturing the attention of hiring managers and securing an interview.

BUILDING A STRONG PROFESSIONAL PROFILE

Tips for Creating an Effective Technical Resume

- Tailor your resume to the specific job requirements, using keywords and phrases from the job description.
- Use a clear and concise format that highlights your technical skills and accomplishments.
- Prioritize your most relevant and impressive technical qualifications and projects.
- Use bullet points and strong action verbs to describe your responsibilities and achievements.
- Quantify your results and impact wherever possible, using metrics and specific examples.
- Keep your resume updated with your latest technical skills, certifications, and projects.
- Proofread your resume carefully to ensure it is error-free and professionally presented.

BUILDING A STRONG PROFESSIONAL PROFILE

I. Resume Format and Appearance

Keep your technical resume simple, clean, and easy to read. Use a clear font like Calibri or Times New Roman, consistent formatting throughout, and bullet points to highlight key information. This will help the reader quickly scan and understand your qualifications.

Maintain a professional appearance with ample white space, clear section headings, and a visually appealing layout. This will make your resume look organized and polished.

Use single spacing within sections and double spacing between sections for improved readability.

BUILDING A STRONG PROFESSIONAL PROFILE

II. Content and Accuracy

Ensure your resume is free of spelling, grammar, and formatting errors. Proofread it carefully and ask someone else to review it and provide feedback. Even small mistakes can create a negative impression.

Provide truthful and accurate information about your skills, experience, and accomplishments. Do not exaggerate or misrepresent your qualifications as this could undermine your credibility.

List your education and work experience in reverse chronological order, starting with your most recent experiences. This allows the reader to quickly see your most up-to-date and relevant information.

III. Tailoring and Customization

Tailor your resume to the specific job requirements. Highlight the technical skills and qualifications that align with the position you're applying for. This will demonstrate your suitability for the role.

BUILDING A STRONG PROFESSIONAL PROFILE

IV. Additional Tips

Keep your resume concise, typically limiting it to one or two pages, depending on your level of experience. Avoid including irrelevant or unnecessary information.

Incorporate relevant technical keywords, strong action verbs, and transferable skills throughout your resume to showcase your capabilities effectively.

Create your resume in a widely accepted format, such as Microsoft Word or PDF, to ensure compatibility and easy sharing.

Avoid including personal information like age, marital status, or religion, and provide references separately upon request.

Write your resume in a professional, third-person style, avoiding the use of personal pronouns like "I," "me," "my," "we," or "our."

Regularly update your resume every six months to include your latest technical skills, certifications, and projects, ensuring it accurately reflects your current qualifications and experiences.

KEY COMPONENTS OF A TECHNICAL RESUME

1. Heading:

- Name: Provide your First Name Last Name on the top of the page.
- Address: Location: Provide your City, State.
- Phone Number: Provide your primary contact phone number.
- Email Address: Provide a professional email address for communication.

2. Profile/Summary of Qualifications:

- Headline: Create a compelling headline that summarizes what you bring to the company.
- Skills: Highlight your key technical skills relevant to the job.
- Qualifications: Emphasize your technical qualifications, certifications, and expertise.
- Accomplishments/Achievements/Awards: Showcase notable technical accomplishments or awards.
- Introduction: Provide a brief introduction that captures your technical expertise and career goals.
- Keywords: Incorporate relevant technical keywords throughout your summary.

KEY COMPONENTS OF A TECHNICAL RESUME

3. Technical Skills Section:

- Highlight your proficiency in programming languages, frameworks, tools, and technologies relevant to your field.
- Use bullet points or a skills matrix to make your technical skills easily scannable.
- Include any certifications or training related to your technical expertise.

4. Projects and Accomplishments:

- Describe technical projects you have worked on, emphasizing your specific role and contributions.
- Use measurable results and metrics to quantify the impact of your work, such as improved efficiency, cost savings, or enhanced security.
- Highlight any innovative solutions or complex challenges you successfully addressed.

KEY COMPONENTS OF A TECHNICAL RESUME

5. Work Experience:

Reverse order: List your work experience starting with the most recent position.

- Company details: Include the company name, city, and state for each position.
- Job Titles and Dates: Specify your job titles and include the month and year for each position.
- Responsibilities: Detail your key responsibilities and tasks in each role.
- Accomplishments: Highlight your technical accomplishments, projects, and measurable results.
- Use technical keywords and industry-specific terminology to demonstrate your familiarity with the field.
- Describe how you applied your technical skills to solve problems, optimize processes, or deliver results.

KEY COMPONENTS OF A TECHNICAL RESUME

6. Education and Certifications:

- List your educational background, including relevant degrees, coursework, and technical training.
- School details: Include the school name, city, and state for each educational institution.
- College focus: If you have college education, focus on that instead of high school information.
- Certifications: Include any relevant technical certifications or training courses.

7. Other:

- Professional affiliations: List any professional organizations or associations you belong to.
- Memberships: Include memberships in relevant technical communities or groups.
- Special awards and recognition: Highlight any notable awards or recognition related to your technical expertise.

WRITING A COMPELLING COVER LETTER

What is a Cover Letter?

A cover letter is a document that accompanies your resume when applying for a job. It serves as an introduction to your resume and provides additional information about your skills, experience, and qualifications. The purpose of a cover letter is to showcase your personality, express your interest in the position and company, and explain why you are the best candidate for the role. It is your first opportunity to make a positive impression on the potential employer and convince them to review your resume.

WRITING A COMPELLING COVER LETTER

How to Write a Compelling Cover Letter

1. Begin with a strong opening paragraph:

- State the position you are applying for and how you learned about the opportunity.
- Express your enthusiasm and interest in the role and the company.
- Briefly mention why you are a strong candidate for the position.

2. Demonstrate your fit for the role:

- Highlight your relevant skills, experience, and qualifications that align with the job requirements.
- Provide specific examples of your accomplishments or projects that demonstrate your abilities.
- Show your knowledge of the company and explain how your values and goals align with their mission.

3. Address the company's specific needs and challenges:

- Research the company and identify their current challenges or objectives.
- Explain how your skills and experience can help them overcome these challenges and achieve their goals.
- Demonstrate your understanding of the industry and the unique value you can bring to the organization.

4. Close with a strong conclusion:

- Express your desire for an interview and propose next steps, such as following up or providing additional information.
- Thank the reader for their time and consideration

OPTIMIZING YOUR LINKEDIN AND HANDSHAKE PROFILES

LinkedIn and Handshake are two powerful online platforms that can help you build your professional network and advance your career in the field of cybersecurity. LinkedIn is the world's largest professional networking site, connecting millions of professionals across various industries. Handshake, on the other hand, is a career platform designed specifically for college students and recent graduates, partnering with universities to help students find job opportunities and connect with potential employers.

To sign up for LinkedIn, visit linkedin.com and click on the "Join now" button. Fill in your personal information, including your name, email address, and a strong password. Once you've created your account, you can start building your profile by adding your education, work experience, skills, and other relevant details.

To create a Handshake account, visit joinhandshake.com and click on the "Sign up" button. Select your university from the list and use your university email address to create your account.
Complete your profile by adding your education, work experience, skills, and other relevant information.

OPTIMIZING YOUR LINKEDIN AND HANDSHAKE PROFILES

To optimize your LinkedIn and Handshake profiles, follow these steps:

1. Choose a professional profile picture: Select a clear, well-lit headshot with a neutral background. Dress in business attire and ensure your face takes up at least 60% of the frame. Use the same profile picture across both platforms for consistency.

2. Craft a compelling headline: Showcase your cybersecurity expertise and career aspirations, including relevant certifications and skills. Keep it concise and under 120 characters. Example: "Aspiring Cybersecurity Analyst | CompTIA Security+ Certified | Passionate about Protecting Digital Assets"

OPTIMIZING YOUR LINKEDIN AND HANDSHAKE PROFILES

4. Detail your education and certifications: Include your degree, major, and any relevant coursework. List your cybersecurity certifications and the year you obtained them, and mention any academic awards, honors, or scholarships.

5. Highlight your relevant experience: Include internships, projects, or volunteer work related to cybersecurity. Use action verbs and quantify your accomplishments when possible, tailoring your experience section to the roles you are targeting.

6. Add skills and seek endorsements: List both technical and soft skills relevant to cybersecurity, including skills mentioned in job descriptions for your target roles. Seek endorsements from colleagues, classmates, or professors who can vouch for your abilities.

7. Customize your profile URL: Create a custom URL for your LinkedIn profile (linkedin.com/in/yourname) and use this URL on your resume, cover letter, and email signature for easy access.

OPTIMIZING YOUR LINKEDIN AND HANDSHAKE PROFILES

To leverage LinkedIn and Handshake for networking:

- Join relevant cybersecurity groups and engage in discussions
- Follow companies of interest and engage with their content
- Connect with alumni and professionals in your desired roles or companies
- Request informational interviews to learn more about career paths and seek advice
- Attend industry events and connect with professionals you meet
- Share industry-related content and add your own commentary to demonstrate your knowledge and engagement

RESEARCHING AND TARGETING COMPANIES

A. Identifying Top Cybersecurity Employers

When researching potential cybersecurity employers, it's essential to consider a diverse range of companies across various industries.

1. Government Agencies:

- National Security Agency (NSA)
- Department of Homeland Security (DHS)
- Federal Bureau of Investigation (FBI)
- Central Intelligence Agency (CIA)
- Department of Defense (DoD)
- National Institute of Standards and Technology (NIST)
- United States Cyber Command (USCYBERCOM)
- Government Accountability Office (GAO)
- Department of Energy (DOE)
- National Aeronautics and Space Administration (NASA)

Government agencies play a crucial role in protecting national security and critical infrastructure. They offer a wide range of cybersecurity positions, from entry-level roles to high-level strategic positions. Working for a government agency can provide unique opportunities to serve your country and gain access to advanced technologies and resources.

RESEARCHING AND TARGETING COMPANIES

2. Consulting Firms:

- Deloitte
- PwC (PricewaterhouseCoopers)
- EY (Ernst & Young)
- KPMG
- Accenture
- Booz Allen Hamilton
- McKinsey & Company
- Boston Consulting Group (BCG)
- Bain & Company
- Protiviti

Consulting firms provide cybersecurity services to a diverse range of clients across various industries. They offer opportunities to work on challenging projects, develop a broad skill set, and gain exposure to different technologies and security frameworks. Consulting firms often have well-established training programs and provide opportunities for career growth and advancement.

RESEARCHING AND TARGETING COMPANIES

3. Cybersecurity Focused Companies:

- CrowdStrike
- FireEye
- Palo Alto Networks
- Broadcom
- Check Point Software Technologies
- Fortinet
- Trend Micro
- McAfee
- Cisco Systems
- Splunk
- RSA Security
- Proofpoint
- Rapid7
- Tenable
- Cloudflare

These companies specialize in providing cybersecurity solutions, products, and services. They are at the forefront of developing innovative technologies to combat cyber threats. Working for a cybersecurity focused company allows you to be part of a team dedicated to solving complex security challenges.

RESEARCHING AND TARGETING COMPANIES

4. Defense Contractors with Cybersecurity Operations:

- Lockheed Martin
- Northrop Grumman
- Raytheon
- Boeing
- General Dynamics
- BAE Systems
- L3Harris Technologies
- Leidos
- CACI International
- Booz Allen Hamilton
- ManTech International
- Science Applications International Corporation (SAIC)
- Parsons Corporation
- Perspecta Inc.
- MITRE Corporation

Defense contractors play a significant role in securing government and military networks and systems. They often have dedicated cybersecurity divisions that work on projects related to national security, cyber warfare, and defense technologies. Working for a defense contractor can provide opportunities to work on high-profile projects and contribute to the protection of critical assets.

RESEARCHING AND TARGETING COMPANIES

5. Healthcare Companies:

- UnitedHealth Group
- McKesson Corporation
- CVS Health
- Anthem Inc.
- Kaiser Permanente
- Cigna Corporation
- Humana Inc.
- HCA Healthcare
- Centene Corporation
- AmerisourceBergen Corporation
- Cardinal Health
- Quest Diagnostics
- LabCorp
- Cerner Corporation
- Epic Systems Corporation

Healthcare companies handle sensitive patient data and are increasingly targeted by cyber threats. They require robust cybersecurity measures to protect electronic health records (EHR), comply with regulations like HIPAA, and ensure the confidentiality and integrity of patient information. Working in the healthcare sector allows you to apply your cybersecurity skills to safeguard critical healthcare systems and protect patient privacy.

RESEARCHING AND TARGETING COMPANIES

B. Strategies for Getting Noticed

To get noticed by top cybersecurity employers, it's important to focus on the skills and requirements you already possess while also demonstrating your desire to learn and grow in the field.

Here are some strategies to help you stand out:

- Emphasize the technical skills and experience you have that align with the company's requirements. If you have hands-on experience with specific cybersecurity tools, technologies, or frameworks, make sure to highlight those in your resume and cover letter.
- Customize your resume and cover letter for each company you apply to, highlighting how your skills and experience match their specific needs and challenges. Demonstrate your knowledge of the company's products, services, and recent developments in the industry.
- Identify experienced professionals in the cybersecurity field who can provide guidance, advice, and support as you navigate your career journey. Reach out to them for informational interviews, seek their feedback on your resume and cover letter, and ask for recommendations on skills to develop or certifications to pursue.
- Demonstrate your genuine interest in cybersecurity by talking about what you find fascinating about the field. Share your thoughts on recent cybersecurity news, trends, or challenges, and discuss how you stay updated with the latest industry developments.

RESEARCHING AND TARGETING COMPANIES

- If you are new to the field or have limited experience, consider applying for junior roles or internships to gain practical experience and build your skills. Many companies offer entry-level positions or internship programs specifically designed for aspiring cybersecurity professionals.
- Participate in cybersecurity conferences, workshops, and networking events to connect with professionals from various companies. Use these opportunities to learn about the latest industry trends, showcase your knowledge, and express your interest in potential job opportunities.
- Follow the company's social media profiles, particularly on LinkedIn and Twitter. Engage with their posts by liking, commenting, and sharing relevant content. Demonstrate your interest in their work and your knowledge of the cybersecurity industry.

RESEARCHING AND TARGETING COMPANIES

Emailing companies directly

One effective strategy for getting noticed by potential employers is to email them directly. Start by identifying relevant contacts within the company, such as hiring managers or cybersecurity team leaders. Craft a personalized email that demonstrates your genuine interest in the company and highlights how your skills and experience align with their needs.

In your email, mention specific projects or initiatives that the company has undertaken that resonate with you, and explain how you could contribute to their success. Attach your tailored resume and a compelling cover letter that showcases your passion for cybersecurity and your fit for the company.

Following them on LinkedIn and engaging with their content

LinkedIn is a powerful platform for getting noticed by potential employers. Follow the company pages of organizations and engage with their content regularly. Like, comment, and share their posts, showcasing your interest in their work and industry insights.

Look for opportunities to contribute to discussions on their posts, offering your perspectives and demonstrating your knowledge of cybersecurity trends and best practices. By actively engaging with their content, you increase your visibility to the company's employees and recruiters.

RESEARCHING AND TARGETING COMPANIES

Leveraging internal referrals and connections

Leveraging internal referrals and connections can significantly increase your chances of getting noticed by potential employers. Reach out to your network, including alumni from your university, former colleagues, and professionals you've met at industry events, and let them know you're seeking new opportunities.

If you have connections within companies like Georgia-Pacific Corporation, Coca-Cola, Home Depot, or any of your target organizations, ask if they would be willing to refer you for relevant positions or provide insights into the company's hiring process. Employee referrals are often given priority by recruiters and can help your application stand out.

Attend industry events, such as conferences and workshops, to expand your network and connect with professionals from your target companies. Engage in meaningful conversations, share your experiences and goals, and follow up with them after the event to maintain the connection and explore potential opportunities.

PREPARING FOR INTERVIEWS

A. Researching the Company and Role

Studying job descriptions thoroughly

Before your cybersecurity interview, thoroughly study the job description to understand the role's requirements and responsibilities. Pay close attention to the specific technical skills, certifications, and experience the employer is seeking. Make a list of the key qualifications and analyze how your background aligns with each one.

Research the company's cybersecurity initiatives, recent projects, and any news or press releases related to their security efforts. Familiarize yourself with the organization's mission, values, and culture. This knowledge will help you tailor your responses and demonstrate your genuine interest in the company.

Aligning your skills and experiences with the requirements

Once you have a clear understanding of the job requirements, identify specific examples from your experiences that demonstrate your proficiency in each area. If the job description emphasizes incident response, think of a time when you successfully handled a security incident and the steps you took to mitigate the threat.

If the role requires experience with specific security tools or technologies, such as SIEM or penetration testing tools, prepare examples of how you have used these tools effectively in your previous roles. By aligning your skills and experiences with the job requirements, you can create a compelling narrative that showcases your fit for the position.

PREPARING FOR INTERVIEWS

B. Developing Your Interview Narrative

Crafting responses

When developing your interview responses, focus on crafting honest, and engaging answers. Start by outlining the key points you want to convey for each question, and practice delivering your responses in a clear and concise manner.

Use the STAR method to structure your answers, providing specific examples that highlight your skills and accomplishments:

- Situation: Describe the context and background of a specific challenge or project you faced. This should include relevant details such as the team you were working with, your role, and the overall goal.
- Task: Explain your specific responsibilities and objectives in that situation. Clearly define what was required of you and what challenges you needed to overcome.
- Action: Describe the actions you took to address the situation and complete the task. This is the most important part of your answer, as it showcases your skills, problem-solving abilities, and initiative. Be specific and provide concrete examples of the steps you took.
- Result: Share the outcomes of your actions. Quantify your results whenever possible, and highlight the impact of your efforts. Explain what you accomplished, what you learned, and how your actions benefited your team or organization.

PREPARING FOR INTERVIEWS

Showcasing your strengths and career evolution

Throughout your interview, focus on showcasing your strengths and the unique qualities that make you stand out as a candidate. Highlight your technical expertise, problem-solving skills, and ability to work collaboratively in a team.

Share examples of how you have continuously learned and adapted to new technologies and cybersecurity challenges throughout your career. Discuss any relevant certifications or training you have pursued to stay up-to-date in the field.

PREPARING FOR INTERVIEWS

Demonstrating your fit for the company culture

In addition to your technical qualifications, it's essential to demonstrate your fit for the company culture. Research the organization's values, mission, and work environment, and prepare examples of how your own values and work style align with theirs.

Share experiences that showcase your ability to collaborate effectively with others. By demonstrating your fit for the company culture, you show the interviewer that you would be a valuable addition.

PREPARING FOR INTERVIEWS

C. Addressing Common Interview Questions

Strengths and Weaknesses

When discussing strengths, highlight qualities directly related to cybersecurity roles, such as:

- Strong technical skills (network security, penetration testing, incident response)
- Analytical and problem-solving abilities for investigating and mitigating threats
- Attention to detail for identifying vulnerabilities and ensuring compliance
- Continuous learning mindset to stay updated on emerging threats/technologies
- Ability to communicate complex technical concepts clearly to non-technical stakeholders

For weaknesses, choose areas not core to the role and explain how you're actively improving, such as:

- Public speaking skills (taking workshops, volunteering for presentations)
- Expertise in a specific cybersecurity domain you're committed to learning

PREPARING FOR INTERVIEWS

Why Should We Hire You?

Focus on highlighting your relevant skills, experiences, and accomplishments that make you a strong candidate for the position. Align your strengths with the key requirements of the role and provide specific examples of how you have applied your skills to solve problems, improve processes, or achieve goals in your previous positions.

Why This Company?

Demonstrate your knowledge and genuine interest in the organization. Research the company's mission, values, and recent developments in advance. Explain how the company's work aligns with your professional goals and values, and express your enthusiasm for contributing to their success.

PREPARING FOR INTERVIEWS

Asking Thoughtful Questions

Prepare insightful questions that show enthusiasm and understanding of their needs:

- What career/professional development opportunities does (Company Name) offer to its employees
- What type of skills is the team missing that you're looking to fill with a new hire?
- How would you describe the company culture at this company?
- What are some of the challenges new hires face during the first 90 days of employment?

CHOOSING THE RIGHT CYBERSECURITY PATH

A. Assessing Your Skills and Interests

Identifying your strengths and preferences

To choose the right cybersecurity career path, begin by assessing your skills and interests. Reflect on your technical abilities, such as programming languages, operating systems, and security tools you are proficient in. Consider your soft skills, like communication, problem-solving, and teamwork, as these are also crucial in the cybersecurity field.

Think about the tasks and projects that you enjoy working on the most. Do you prefer hands-on technical work, such as configuring security systems and analyzing malware? Or do you enjoy interacting with people, educating others about security best practices, and managing projects? Identifying your strengths and preferences will help you narrow down the cybersecurity roles that align best with your skills and interests.

CHOOSING THE RIGHT CYBERSECURITY PATH

Aligning your skills with different cybersecurity roles

Once you have identified your strengths and preferences, research the various cybersecurity roles and their requirements. Compare your skills and interests with the responsibilities and qualifications of each role.

For example, if you have strong programming skills and enjoy problem-solving, you may be well-suited for a role as a security software developer or a penetration tester.

Consider taking online assessments or career aptitude tests specific to the cybersecurity field. These tools can provide valuable insights into your strengths and suggest roles that align with your skills and interests.

CHOOSING THE RIGHT CYBERSECURITY PATH

B. Exploring Various Cybersecurity Roles

Consulting and sales for people-oriented professionals

If you enjoy interacting with people and have strong communication and problem-solving skills, cybersecurity consulting and sales roles may be a good fit. As a cybersecurity consultant, you would work with clients to assess their security needs, develop strategies, and implement solutions to protect their assets.

In a sales engineering role, you would collaborate with sales teams to provide technical expertise, demonstrate security products, and help clients understand how the solutions can address their specific security challenges. These roles require a combination of technical knowledge and excellent interpersonal skills to effectively communicate with clients and build strong relationships.

CHOOSING THE RIGHT CYBERSECURITY PATH

Security administration, digital forensics, or security engineering for technical experts

For those with strong technical skills and a passion for hands-on work, security administration, digital forensics, and security engineering roles offer exciting opportunities. As a security administrator, you would be responsible for managing and maintaining an organization's security systems, such as firewalls, intrusion detection systems, and access control mechanisms.

Digital forensics professionals investigate cyber incidents and gather evidence to support legal proceedings. They use specialized tools and techniques to recover and analyze data from compromised systems and devices.

Security engineers design, implement, and maintain an organization's security infrastructure. They develop secure architectures, configure security tools, and monitor systems for vulnerabilities and threats. These roles require a deep understanding of security technologies and a strong foundation in computer science and networking.

CHOOSING THE RIGHT CYBERSECURITY PATH

Penetration testing, auditing, or vulnerability assessment for those who love hacking

If you have a passion for hacking and enjoy the challenge of identifying and exploiting vulnerabilities, penetration testing, auditing, and vulnerability assessment roles may be the perfect fit. As a penetration tester, you would simulate real-world attacks to evaluate the effectiveness of an organization's security controls. You would use a variety of tools and techniques to identify weaknesses and provide recommendations for remediation.

Auditors review an organization's security policies, procedures, and controls to ensure compliance with industry standards and regulations. They assess the overall security posture and provide recommendations for improvement.

Vulnerability assessment professionals scan networks, systems, and applications to identify potential vulnerabilities and misconfigurations. They prioritize risks and provide guidance on remediation strategies to mitigate identified weaknesses.

These roles require a deep understanding of hacking techniques, a creative mindset, and the ability to think like an attacker. Ethical hacking certifications, such as the Certified Ethical Hacker or Offensive Security Certified Professional, can demonstrate your skills and knowledge in this area.

When choosing your cybersecurity career path, consider your long-term goals and the potential for growth and advancement within each role. Research the career trajectories of professionals in your desired field and identify the skills and certifications that are most valuable for progression.

JOB SEARCH STRATEGIES AND RESOURCES

A. Leveraging Job Search Platforms

Leveraging General Job Search Platforms

Flexjobs, Linkedin, Indeed, and Google for Jobs are popular job search websites that aggregate listings from various sources across multiple industries. These platforms allow you to set up customized job alerts based on your preferred roles, locations, and keywords, ensuring you receive notifications about new opportunities that match your criteria. While not exclusively focused on cybersecurity, these sites can be valuable resources for exploring a wide range of job postings from diverse employers.

Utilizing Niche Cybersecurity Job Boards

For a more targeted approach, explore specialized job boards that cater specifically to the cybersecurity field. The ISACA Career Centre Job Board, provided by the Information Systems Audit and Control Association, is a niche platform that focuses on roles in information systems audit, control, and security. This board can be a valuable resource for professionals seeking cybersecurity positions within this specific domain.

JOB SEARCH STRATEGIES AND RESOURCES

Exploring Entry-Level and Government Opportunities

For those just starting their cybersecurity careers, WayUp is a platform that connects recent graduates with entry-level jobs and internships, making it a valuable resource for gaining initial experience. If interested in government positions, USAJOBS is the official job site of the U.S. federal government, offering cybersecurity roles within various agencies, including the Department of Homeland Security's Cybersecurity Service.

Specialized Cybersecurity Job Boards

Several job boards are dedicated exclusively to the cybersecurity field, providing a highly targeted approach to job searching. CyberSecJobs.com, Infosec-Jobs.com, JobTome.com, and CareersInCyber.com are examples of platforms that curate job listings from various companies and organizations specifically within the cybersecurity domain. These specialized boards can be invaluable for finding opportunities that closely align with your cybersecurity skills and career aspirations.

JOB SEARCH STRATEGIES AND RESOURCES

B. Tailoring Your Applications

Customizing your resume and cover letter for each job

To stand out in a competitive job market, it's essential to tailor your resume and cover letter for each job application. Start by thoroughly reviewing the job description and identifying the key skills, qualifications, and experience the employer is seeking.

Customize your resume by highlighting the most relevant aspects of your background that align with the job requirements. Use similar language and keywords from the job description to demonstrate your fit for the role. Adapt your professional summary and work experience bullets to emphasize the skills and accomplishments that are most applicable to the position.

Similarly, craft a targeted cover letter that showcases your interest in the specific role and company. Demonstrate your knowledge of the organization and explain how your skills and experience make you an ideal candidate for the position. Use specific examples to illustrate your qualifications and tie them back to the job requirements.

JOB SEARCH STRATEGIES AND RESOURCES

Highlighting specific keywords and skills from the job description

Many companies use applicant tracking systems to screen resumes and cover letters for relevant keywords and qualifications. To increase your chances of passing through these automated filters, incorporate specific keywords and skills from the job description into your application materials.

Identify the most important technical skills, certifications, and experience mentioned in the job posting, and ensure that they are prominently featured in your resume and cover letter. Use the same language and terminology as the job description to optimize your materials for ATS compatibility.

However, be cautious not to overuse keywords. Your application should still read naturally and demonstrate your genuine qualifications for the role. Use keywords strategically and in context to showcase your relevant skills and experience.

JOB SEARCH STRATEGIES AND RESOURCES

C. Networking and Building Relationships

Attending industry events and conferences

Networking is a critical component of any successful job search strategy. Attend cybersecurity industry events and conferences to connect with professionals, learn about the latest trends and technologies, and discover potential job opportunities.

Look for events hosted by professional associations, such as the Information Systems Security Association, the International Information System Security Certification Consortium (ISC)[2], and the ISACA. These organizations often host local chapter meetings, workshops, and conferences that provide valuable networking opportunities.

When attending events, engage in meaningful conversations with other attendees. Share your background, interests, and career goals, and ask about their experiences and insights. Exchange contact information and follow up after the event to maintain the connection and explore potential collaborations or job leads.

JOB SEARCH STRATEGIES AND RESOURCES

Joining online communities and forums

Engage with online communities and forums focused on cybersecurity to expand your network and stay informed about industry trends and job opportunities. Platforms like Reddit, Discord, and Slack have active cybersecurity communities where professionals share knowledge, discuss challenges, and support one another.

Participate in discussions, ask questions, and share your insights to establish yourself as an active and knowledgeable member of the community. Contribute to conversations about the latest cybersecurity news, tools, and best practices to demonstrate your expertise and passion for the field.

Many online communities also have job boards or channels where members share open positions and career opportunities. Monitor these resources regularly and engage with members who post about job openings that align with your interests and qualifications.

JOB SEARCH STRATEGIES AND RESOURCES

Engaging with professionals on social media

Social media platforms like LinkedIn and Twitter provide excellent opportunities to connect with cybersecurity professionals and engage in industry conversations. Follow thought leaders, influencers, and companies in the cybersecurity space to stay informed about the latest trends and insights.

Share relevant articles, news, and resources with your network to demonstrate your knowledge and interest in the field. Engage with others' posts by commenting, asking questions, and sharing your perspectives. This helps establish your presence and credibility within the cybersecurity community.

Use LinkedIn to connect with professionals in your desired roles or companies. Personalize your connection requests by mentioning shared interests or experiences, and express your interest in learning more about their work and career paths. Once connected, engage in meaningful conversations and seek advice on breaking into the field or advancing your career.

JOB SEARCH STRATEGIES AND RESOURCES

Twitter is another valuable platform for engaging with the cybersecurity community. Participate in relevant hashtags and discussions, share your thoughts and experiences, and connect with professionals who share your interests. Many cybersecurity experts and organizations use Twitter to share job postings, so keep an eye out for potential opportunities.

Remember to maintain a professional online presence across all social media platforms. Ensure that your profiles and content reflect your skills, experience, and passion for cybersecurity. Regularly update your profiles with your latest achievements, certifications, and projects to showcase your continuous learning and growth in the field.

NEGOTIATING JOB OFFERS AND COMPENSATION

A. Researching Salary Benchmarks

Understanding market rates for your skills and experience

Before entering into any job offer negotiations, it's crucial to research and understand the market rates for your specific skills, experience level, and location. This knowledge will help you determine a fair and competitive compensation package and provide a foundation for your negotiation strategy.

Start by exploring salary benchmarking resources specific to the cybersecurity industry. Websites like PayScale, Glassdoor, and the Bureau of Labor Statistics offer salary data based on job titles, years of experience, and geographic location. Use these resources to gather data on the average base salary, bonuses, and other compensation components for roles similar to the one you are considering.

In addition to online resources, leverage your professional network to gain insights into salary expectations. Reach out to mentors, colleagues, or alumni from your cybersecurity program who are working in similar roles or companies. Ask for their advice on fair compensation ranges and negotiation strategies based on their experiences.

NEGOTIATING JOB OFFERS AND COMPENSATION

Utilizing salary comparison tools and resources

Take advantage of salary comparison tools and resources to gain a more comprehensive understanding of market rates. These tools allow you to input specific job titles, locations, and experience levels to generate detailed salary reports.

Some popular salary comparison resources include:

- PayScale: Provides a free salary survey that generates a personalized salary report based on your job title, location, experience, and other factors.
- Glassdoor: Offers user-submitted salary data for specific companies and job titles, as well as insights into company cultures and interview processes.
- LinkedIn Salary: Allows users to access salary data based on job title, location, and years of experience, as well as compare salaries across different companies and industries.
- Cybersecurity Salary Calculator (https://www.cyberseek.org/pathway.html): A tool specifically designed for the cybersecurity industry, providing salary ranges for various roles based on location and experience level.

NEGOTIATING JOB OFFERS AND COMPENSATION

Considering non-salary benefits and perks

While base salary is a primary component of any compensation package, it's important to consider non-salary benefits and perks that can significantly impact your overall job satisfaction and financial well-being.

During the negotiation process, inquire about the company's benefits package, including health insurance, retirement plans, paid time off, and professional development opportunities. Assess how these benefits align with your personal and professional goals and factor them into your decision-making process.

Consider negotiating for additional perks that are valuable to you, such as flexible work arrangements, telework options, or educational reimbursements for cybersecurity certifications or conferences. These non-salary benefits can often be more easily negotiated than base salary and can greatly enhance your overall compensation package.

NEGOTIATING JOB OFFERS AND COMPENSATION

Maintaining professionalism and respect throughout the process

Throughout the negotiation process, it's crucial to maintain professionalism and respect for all parties involved. Approach the discussion with a collaborative and solution-oriented mindset, focusing on finding a mutually beneficial outcome.

Express your gratitude for the job offer and the opportunity to discuss compensation. Use positive and assertive language when communicating your expectations and counter-offers.

Be prepared to justify your salary expectations based on your research and the value you bring to the company. If the employer is unable to meet your initial request, consider alternative options, such as a signing bonus, performance-based incentives, or a commitment to revisit compensation after a certain period of time.

If you are considering multiple job offers, be transparent with the employers about your timeline and decision-making process. Avoid using competing offers as leverage unless you are genuinely interested in the other opportunities and willing to accept them if negotiations fall through.

NEGOTIATING JOB OFFERS AND COMPENSATION

Remember that the negotiation process is an opportunity to build a positive relationship with your future employer. Even if you do not reach an agreement on all aspects of the compensation package, maintain a professional and respectful demeanor. Your conduct during the negotiation process can set the tone for your future working relationship and reputation within the industry.

Negotiating job offers and compensation can be a challenging and intimidating process, but by conducting thorough research, communicating your value, and maintaining professionalism, you can secure a competitive and fair compensation package that recognizes your skills and contributions to the cybersecurity field.

DEVELOPING A CUSTOMIZED CAREER ACTION PLAN

A. Setting clear and achievable career goals

To effectively launch your cybersecurity career, it's crucial to develop a customized career action plan that outlines your goals, strategies, and the steps you will take to achieve success. The first step in creating your action plan is to set clear and achievable career goals that align with your interests, skills, and aspirations.

Short-term objectives

Begin by defining your short-term objectives, which are the goals you aim to achieve within the next 6 to 12 months. These objectives should be specific, measurable, achievable, relevant, and time-bound (SMART).

Examples of short-term objectives may include:

- Obtaining a relevant cybersecurity certification
- Gaining hands-on experience through an internship or entry-level position in a cybersecurity role
- Building a strong professional network by attending industry events and engaging with the cybersecurity community
- Developing a portfolio of projects that showcase your technical skills and practical experience

DEVELOPING A CUSTOMIZED CAREER ACTION PLAN

Long-term aspirations

In addition to short-term objectives, it's important to define your long-term aspirations, which are the goals you hope to achieve over the next 3 to 5 years. These aspirations should align with your overall career vision and reflect the impact you want to make in the field of cybersecurity.

Examples of long-term aspirations may include:
-
- Progressing to a senior or leadership role within a cybersecurity team
- Specializing in a specific domain, such as penetration testing, incident response, or cloud security
- Contributing to the cybersecurity community through research, publications, or speaking engagements
- Pursuing advanced certifications or a graduate degree in cybersecurity to deepen your expertise

DEVELOPING A CUSTOMIZED CAREER ACTION PLAN

B. Creating a timeline and milestones

Once you have defined your career goals, the next step is to create a timeline and establish milestones to guide your progress and keep you on track.

Breaking down goals into actionable steps

Break down each of your short-term objectives and long-term aspirations into smaller, actionable steps. These steps should be specific tasks or activities that you can complete to move closer to your goals. For example, if your short-term objective is to obtain a cybersecurity certification, the actionable steps may include:

- Researching and selecting the appropriate certification based on your career goals and job market demands
- Enrolling in a certification preparation course or study program
- Allocating dedicated study time and creating a study schedule
- Practicing with mock exams and hands-on labs to reinforce your knowledge and skills
- Scheduling and taking the certification exam

Establishing deadlines and tracking progress

Assign realistic deadlines to each actionable step and milestone to create a sense of urgency and accountability. Use a calendar, planner, or project management tool to track your progress and ensure that you are staying on schedule. Regularly review your progress and adjust your timeline as needed based on your achievements or any unforeseen challenges.

DEVELOPING A CUSTOMIZED CAREER ACTION PLAN

C. Identifying resources and support needed

To successfully execute your career action plan, it's important to identify the resources and support you will need along the way.

Training and certifications

Determine the specific training and certifications that will help you achieve your career goals and enhance your marketability in the job market. Research reputable training providers, online courses, and certification programs that align with your learning style and budget. Consider factors such as the curriculum, instructor quality, hands-on labs, and industry recognition when selecting training and certification options.

Mentorship and guidance

Seek mentorship and guidance from experienced professionals in the cybersecurity field who can provide valuable insights, advice, and support as you navigate your career journey. Identify potential mentors within your professional network, industry associations, or through mentorship programs offered by cybersecurity organizations. Establish regular communication with your mentors and be proactive in seeking their guidance on career decisions, skill development, and overcoming challenges.

DEVELOPING A CUSTOMIZED CAREER ACTION PLAN

Financial planning and budgeting

Consider the financial implications of pursuing your career goals and develop a budget to support your action plan. Factor in costs such as training and certification fees, conferences and event attendance, professional membership dues, and any necessary equipment or software investments. Explore options for financial assistance, such as employer-sponsored training programs, scholarships, or grants offered by cybersecurity organizations or educational institutions.

OVERCOMING OBSTACLES & STAYING MOTIVATED

A. Addressing imposter syndrome and self-doubt

As you embark on your cybersecurity career, it's common to experience imposter syndrome and self-doubt. Imposter syndrome is the feeling of inadequacy and self-doubt despite evidence of your accomplishments and capabilities. It can make you question your skills, knowledge, and belonging in the field. However, it's crucial to recognize that imposter syndrome is a normal experience and that you are not alone in facing these feelings.

Recognizing your achievements and progress

To combat imposter syndrome, take the time to acknowledge and celebrate your achievements and progress. Reflect on the skills you have acquired, the projects you have completed, and the challenges you have overcome. Keep a record of your accomplishments, positive feedback, and milestones reached. Regularly review this record to remind yourself of your growth and capabilities when self-doubt creeps in.

Embracing a growth mindset

Adopt a growth mindset, which is the belief that your abilities and intelligence can be developed through dedication and hard work. Embrace the idea that challenges and setbacks are opportunities for learning and growth. When faced with self-doubt, reframe your thoughts to focus on the progress you have made and the potential for further development. Seek constructive feedback, learn from your mistakes, and view failures as stepping stones to success.

OVERCOMING OBSTACLES & STAYING MOTIVATED

B. Dealing with job search challenges and rejections

The job search process in the cybersecurity field can be challenging, and rejections are a common part of the experience. It's important to develop strategies to cope with these challenges and maintain a positive outlook.

Persevering through setbacks

Recognize that setbacks and rejections are a normal part of the job search process and do not define your worth or capabilities. Persevere through these challenges by maintaining a resilient mindset and focusing on your long-term goals. Treat each setback as an opportunity to learn and improve your job search strategies. Continue to apply for positions, network with professionals, and refine your skills.

Learning from feedback and experiences

When faced with rejections or unsuccessful interviews, seek feedback from the employers or hiring managers. Ask for constructive criticism on your application, interview performance, or areas for improvement. Use this feedback to identify gaps in your skills or experience and develop a plan to address them. Reflect on your job search experiences and evaluate what strategies have been effective and where you can make adjustments.

OVERCOMING OBSTACLES & STAYING MOTIVATED

C. Maintaining motivation and passion for cybersecurity

Maintaining motivation and passion for cybersecurity is essential for long-term success and fulfillment in your career. Here are some strategies to help you stay motivated and engaged:

Engaging in continuous learning and skill development

Continuously invest in your learning and skill development to stay motivated and up-to-date with the latest trends and technologies in the field. Pursue certifications, attend workshops and conferences, and engage in hands-on projects that challenge you and expand your knowledge. Embrace the mindset of a lifelong learner and seek opportunities to explore new areas of cybersecurity that align with your interests and career goals.

Surrounding yourself with a supportive network

Build a supportive network of mentors, colleagues, and professionals who share your passion for cybersecurity. Engage with online communities, attend industry events, and participate in professional associations to connect with like-minded individuals. Surround yourself with people who inspire and motivate you, offer guidance and support, and celebrate your successes. Having a strong support system can help you stay motivated and overcome challenges throughout your career journey.

OVERCOMING OBSTACLES & STAYING MOTIVATED

Celebrating small victories and milestones

Recognize and celebrate the small victories and milestones along your career path. Acknowledge your progress, whether it's completing a challenging project, earning a certification, or receiving positive feedback from a colleague or supervisor. Take the time to reflect on your achievements and share your successes with your support network. Celebrating these victories, no matter how small, can boost your motivation and provide a sense of accomplishment.

CONCLUSION

Thanks for allowing me to provide you the game on Cybersecurity. We kicked things off by learning cybersecurity fundamentals, breaking down the different domains and career paths you can take. We made sure you're up to date with the latest trends and threats. Next, we covered all the essential principles, policies, and frameworks you need to know.

From there, we got into the fundamentals of security operations. We talked about data security, system hardening, and why security awareness training is so crucial. We also explored networking concepts, so you can understand how to keep systems secure.

You've learned to think like a hacker, understanding their motives and how they plan their attacks. By getting inside their heads, you're now better prepared to defend against whatever they throw your way.

We also showed you how to utilize Linux and Python to automate and streamline your security tasks. You've gotten hands-on experience with system administration, asset management, and how Active Directory and Group Policy play a big role in keeping IT environments secure.

Through a multi-layered approach to defense, you've learned how to set up firewalls, intrusion prevention systems, and lock down access controls. We also explained the complexities of offensive security, where you learned about web application vulnerabilities, penetration testing, and the art of social engineering.

CONCLUSION

You've developed some skills in incident response, digital forensics, and the NIST Cybersecurity Framework. We also helped you navigate cybersecurity certifications, so you can choose the right path for your career.

Most importantly, you've developed important skills. You've set up virtual labs, analyzed packets, hardened systems, and configured firewalls.

Throughout this journey, you've also sharpened your professional skills. You've learned how to build a strong profile, research potential employers, and crush your interviews. You know how to showcase your skills and stay motivated even when things get tough.

As you navigate cybersecurity, remember that this is just the beginning. This field is always evolving and broad, so your commitment to continuous learning and growth will be the key to your success.

I hope that Cybersecurity Masterclass has given you the knowledge, skills, and confidence to launch your career. We can't wait to see the impact you'll. Let's go!

ABOUT THE AUTHOR

Tony Evans is a cybersecurity expert, educator, and author with a passion for guiding Cybersecurity professionals. After earning his Master's Degree in Cybersecurity from Kennesaw State University, Tony quickly discovered the challenges of navigating the field. Determined to help others avoid common struggles, Tony has dedicated his career to breaking down the complexities of Cybersecurity into clear, actionable steps.

Today, Tony leverages his real-world experience, both in the industry and as a cybersecurity instructor at Chattahoochee Tech, to empower students and professionals with the tools and knowledge they need to succeed.

As the founder of PROFYLE PUBLISHING LLC, Tony is committed to creating accessible, high-quality resources that help people break into the Cybersecurity field with confidence. His goal is to show professionals that success in Cybersecurity comes from mastering key skills, earning certifications, and building a standout social profile. Tony's mission is to inspire, motivate, and equip his audience with the knowledge to not only master the technical aspects of Cybersecurity but also thrive in their careers.

PROFYLE PUBLISHING offers both Standard and Premium Opportunities, helping professionals at every stage of their journey. The Standard Package provides essential tools like resume and cover letter templates, job search strategies, and career-building resources. For those looking to go further, the Premium Grand Package offer personalized coaching, resume enhancement services, LinkedIn profile optimization, and exclusive access to the tools needed to fast-track a successful Cybersecurity career.